FLESH OF GOD:
THE SACRED MUSHROOM TRADITION OF THE MAZATEC SHAMANS

ENRIQUE GONZÁLEZ RUBIO MONTOYA
Translated by
Eugenia Wolstein and
Angel Silva

ARKA

The content of this book is for informational purposes only and is not intended to diagnose, treat, cure, or prevent any condition or disease. You understand that this book is not intended as a substitute for consultation with a licensed practitioner. Please consult with your own physician or healthcare specialist regarding the suggestions and recommendations made in this book. The use of this book implies your acceptance of this disclaimer.

Copyright © by Enrique González Rubio Montoya.

Edited by Christian Ortiz.

www.casaarka.com

All rights reserved. This book or parts thereof may not be reproduced in any form, stored in any retrieval system, or transmitted in any form by any means—electronic, mechanical, photocopy, recording, or otherwise—without prior written permission of the publisher

Thanks to Eugenia Wolstein for the first version of this book in English.
With sincere gratitude to Angel Silva for the translation of this book, his friendship and support during the process of publication.
With appreciation to Dr. Marian Reiff for the final version of the manuscript.

"I ask you, oh priests:
From where do the intoxicating flowers come?
And the seductive songs come only from His house in Heaven,
And from his Heaven also come the scented blossoms.
Let it said that there are flowery songs.
Let them say that I drink heady flowers.
The flowers that exhilarate are now here.
Come all of you, and be blessed"
Nahuatl poem

CONTENT

Introduction
Prologue

PART 1: MARÍA SABINA AND OTHER HEALERS

Huautla, the Eagle´s Lair... 18
Teonanacatl, Flesh of God...22
In Hell and in Heaven..28
Maria Sabina..31
The Gnome..38
Don Ernesto...41
Pablo..45
The Mushroom Ceremony...53
The Gods...57
Communion with the Spirits..60
Nahualism..64
Philosophy, Psychology and Telepathy...66
Don Ricardo, The Healer from Santa Cruz...70
The Dream to an Enchanted Place..72
Death of Maria Sabina..74
Remembering of Maria Sabina...78
Spiritual Solitude and Mysticism..83
Worshiping the Eternal Father 85
Healing Prayers...88
Songs of Maria Sabina..94

PART 2: THE MAGIC OF THE MAZATEC SHAMANS

The Shaman or Eagle Warrior...96
The magic Hummingbird..100
The wonders of the Mazatec Sierra...102
Twelve Clans of Eagle Warriors..104
Doña Julieta, the Eagle Warrior...106
The Holy Children...111
The Earth Spirits: Chicon Nangui..116
Thunder Mountain: Nindo Chinkao...120
The Mountain of Worship..124
The white Dog of Chicon...127
Joaquin...130
 Dream and Magic...133
The Nahual on the way to Tuxtepec..137
The Lords of the water..139
The Witches of San Mateo..141
The Weed Cat..145
The Stone of the Gnomes..147
The Magic Hut..148
The Joining of Joaquin and Maria Sabina..151
All Saints' Day: a Ritual from Beyond...153
The day the Mountain Spoke to Me...160
Ceremony in Heaven..162
Plants that Teach Wisdom..168
Glorious Dawn...172
The Power of Faith, Prayer and Fasting..174
Journey through the Solar System..176
A New Eagle Warrior..179
To Foreign Lands..180
Special Interview (PODCAST)...186

WARNING

All researchers into Mexican Indian magic must exercise care in the selection of topics to study. There are great masters who practice healing, but unfortunately, there are also many charlatans and worse, there are masters in the black arts passing themselves off as healers. Many started out with good intentions but turned away from the highest ideals of healing.

The magic of the sacred mushroom is dangerous ground. It involves the passage into an unknown country where the neophyte is at disadvantage. Without the knowledge of the necessary rituals, he or she has to confront phenomena which are out of his/her control.

The mushrooms are neither good nor bad, it all depends what use is made of them. The danger is that there are wolves pretending to be lambs among those who present themselves as healers. One has to be quite careful as the consequences can lead to insanity and death. The path of the researcher must be walked with care and respect.

An integral part of this approach is to maintain the necessary seriousness of purpose and integrity in the face of the unknown. The researcher must be totally free of any preconceptions or theoretical frameworks which pigeonhole the experience of the mushroom, and prevent the needed objectivity of understanding the indigenous magic.

INTRODUCTION

I was an Anthropology student in Mexico City specializing in the field of shamanism, and I decided to do my thesis and field practice about the ceremonial uses of the sacred mushrooms called *"Teonanacatl"* (word from the Nahuatl language that means "Flesh of God"), also called "The Holy Children" –practiced by the Mazatec, one of the indigenous groups in the state of Oaxaca, Mexico. These practices are part of the cultural richness of the pre-Hispanic past of Mexico, but are still alive.

This writing is the narration of my ritual experiences with Mazatec shamans. Some of the main aspects of my experiences as a participant in these rituals were: Mystical ecstasy, enlightenment, as well as paranormal psychic phenomena, such as telepathy, clairvoyance, magnetism (healing touch). I was also an eyewitness of indigenous traditional medicine healing, through the mushrooms Ceremony, with shamanic chants and prayer.

The ceremonies of the sacred mushrooms, involved a direct interface with the world of the sacred –until then unknown to me and this caused me to re-evaluate of my concepts as to the meaning of the universe and my understanding of myself as a human being.

As part of my research, I had the privilege of meeting with the famous Mazatec shaman Maria Sabina, known worldwide as "the Priestess of the Magic Mushrooms", after the publication of Gordon Wasson´s monographs, during the 60´s, and also to participate several times in her Ceremony of the mushrooms.

My meetings with Maria Sabina and her ceremonies had a deep importance for me; it changed totally the meaning of my existence and my perception of the world. I learned deeper and higher things from this wise and humble indigenous shaman than all the books and professors of Anthropology School, with their atheist Marxism could teach me.

Maria Sabina, through her Ceremony and her shamanic chants, led me to the presence of God! My experience with her was sublime, spiritual. Because of that I decided to write this book, to share with the world the wonders of this spiritual wisdom that I learned from the Mazatec shamans.

When I finished my manuscript, I gave it to one of my professors in the Anthropology School, to get her approval and to present it as my thesis. The professor, after reading it, told me:

"-Enrique, your manuscript is really interesting, I congratulate you, but the professor will not accept it as your thesis, because it is not written in a scientific way. You are not an anthropologist, you are a writer."

After several days meditating about this matter, I understood that she was right.

I decided to forget about Anthropology and Science, and to dedicate myself to Literature, and to seek the indigenous spiritual wisdom. I think it was a good decision: As anthropologist, I was forced to adapt myself to the way of thinking and interpretation of the professors; as a writer, I felt free to think and write whatever my conscience dictated to me.

What I discovered in the mountains was a challenge to all the scientific ideas that I was learning at the Anthropology School. I was in a deep philosophical dilemma: To keep the perception of the world that I learned from the professors, or to open my mind to the spiritual understanding of the universe that I received from the shamans. I decided to receive the sacred knowledge, even knowing that this decision would separate my consciousness from the ideology of all my professors. This was not an easy choice. But I am sure I made the right decision. I became not a student of Anthropology anymore, but an student of indigenous sacred knowledge (shamanism).

Through the ceremonies, the shaman or healer gets the awareness of the spiritual consciousness and the acquisition of the so called hidden powers of the mind, such as clairvoyance, telepathy and healing touch.

During several years my consciousness had been sleeping. My experiences with the shamanic Ceremonies made wake up and become aware that humans are not just a body and a mind, we are something else, and our real essence is divine and spiritual.

The discovery of this truth was something really important, I couldn't keep quiet, I felt the need to write about what I found, to share it with others, to say them: "I found that we are spiritual beings, God is real, is present in each particle of the universe, as well as within each of us."

This is the essence of the sacred knowledge that I found among the shamans, in the Mazatec mountains. This knowledge must be justly valued, because it is part of the spiritual inheritance of humankind.

Destiny led me to become a spokesman of indigenous shamanic knowledge. The main idea of this writing is to share my testimony about super-natural experiences –or paranormal, according to parapsychology- and miraculous healing –at least without an explanation in current science.

The goal is to preserve this knowledge before the Mazatec become integrated into modern society, and lose their cultural identity. Before to write this book, I asked their permission to Maria Sabina and the other shamans, and all of them accepted.

The value that this writing can have is to be a truthful testimony. This is not literary fiction: all the characters and events are authentic.

The mystery and greatness of the Ceremonies touched my consciousness causing me to write this book; as one way to share the spiritual wonders that I found. The shamanic Mazatec knowledge is part of the indigenous cultural inheritance of Mexico, and I believe that it has universal value.

This writing is not an anthropologic study about indigenous magic, but the testimony of a conversion: from an Anthropology student, to a seeker of the spiritual wisdom hidden in the mountains of the Mazatec Sierra.

PROLOGUE

Mazatecah is a word from the Nahuatl language which means People of Mazatlan. *Mazatl* means deer, *tlan* means place. Mazatlan means therefore "place where deer abound."

Mazatecah has been adapted to the Spanish language and is now applied as feminine or masculine adjective, *mazateco* o *mazateca.*

The Mazateca population is comprised of the Zapotecs and Popolocas. Their language is a derivative of the Popoloca.

The origins of the Mazatecs are very old; we do not have as much knowledge of their history as we do for other cultures. That may be a reason that it has been the subject of study by so many anthropologists.

Many of the studies however seem to have a Marxist bent which leads them away from the magic character of their religion and beliefs.

The Mazatecs live in the mountains of the Mexican sates of Oaxaca, Puebla and Veracruz. They were fierce fighters expertly using extremely long lances in combat. Nevertheless, they were conquered by the Mixtecas and later by the Mexica. When the Spaniards established their hegemony, the Indian population was decimated due in great part to the exploitation of the workforce but also to the European diseases to which the Indians were vulnerable.

There are less than 300,000 Mazatecs today and they continue to inhabit their traditional homeland. Although the topography is so varied that it comprises land at sea-level and the high sierra with altitudes of up to 2,500 meters, the majority live in the mountains and the valleys.

The irregularity of their homeland is the cause of so much difference in the vegetation and the climate, as well as their habits and the barrier to ongoing communication. In addition, more than sixty per cent of the Mazatec speak only their language.

Their homeland is also rich in minerals, like antimony, basalt, pyrite, quartz, obsidian and marble. Their woods produce fine wood for furniture and are also the home for varied fauna, which includes deer, hare, and fox. There are also many flesh eating birds, particularly vultures, eagles and hawks.

The Mazatecs have two types of houses, for cold climate and hot. Those in the cold climate use primarily a rectangular structure, six meters in length by four in width. The walls are high and generally made of adobe or stone. Some are made of wood, mainly reed, covered with thick mud, the roof is made of palm leaves or hay, and with the advent of civilization, and they have begun to use water resistant cardboard or metal sheets.

The houses in the hot climates are generally round and the roofs are covered with leaves from sugar cane or palm.

The most traditional wear for these people is the gala dress for women which are reserved for fiestas. It is a knee length *huipil* made of fine cotton, and it is decorated with colored ribbons running lengthwise. The bust is embroidered with beautiful and colorful figures of animals, often birds and eagles. Also, the *huipil* is completed in the lower part with a broad swath in red thread followed by a long skirt that reaches the ankles. They comb their hair with oil from the seed of the *mamey,* and they make two long pigtails with colorful ribbon adorning them. When they go out, they wear a dark *rebozo* for protection although it is also a very colorful and elegant.

They like to wear jewelry, mainly rings and ear rings made of gold or silver. The daily dress is simple and unadorned, made from white cotton.

Men wear white cotton pants and shirt, huaraches and sombreros (hats), often a machete hanging from the waist.

Coffee is the usual product of their economy, and often it is of good quality. Their religious life is reach and varied. They have a great knowledge of healing herbs which goes back many generations.

Pregnant women in their fourth month are usually given massage to ensure that the womb is properly placed. In the eight month, the healer begins to propitiate the gods and massages a mixture of tobacco and lime juice on the arms of the mother to be in order to protect her from evil doers. A midwife usually attends at birth.

When they harvest the first earn of corn they sprinkle it with blood from a female turkey and they burn it as an offering to the lord of the mountain, a very important god in their pantheon whom they call *"Chicon Nindo Tocosho."*

The Lord of the Mountain is venerated throughout by the healers who attribute to him their power to heal and to see into the psyche of the patient by means of the mushroom.

The Lord of the Mountain also governs the *"owners of the land"*, who also live in the mountains, and who are propitiated with cacao beans as gifts to gain their favor.

The Mazatecs also recognize the existence of the *Nahual* (an evil person or spirit) but attribute to them an evil bent which leads to illness among the unguarded.

The most important fiestas are religious in nature, the highest observance being All Saints' Day on the second of November.

Although the Mazatecs are catholic, they retain many other pre-Columbian beliefs without experiencing any inconsistency in their devotion to both. The many customs which they have retained give us an accurate glimpse into their belief system, particularly regarding the use of the mushroom in the pre-Hispanic world.

The shamanic tradition of the Mazatecs saw its beginnings in antiquity, possibly going back to the Toltec and the Olmec. The shamanic songs speak of the religious spirit of the American inhabitants who have kept their most sacred traditions intact in spite of the often brutal Spanish conquest and colonization. Christianity has changed the physical aspect of the mushroom Ceremony but the intrinsic belief in the Indian god scheme has not changed, particularly among those healers who have remained detached from western-style civilization.

The Mazatecs still live with an attitude that the world is magical and sacred. The magic of the mushroom is so vast and complex that no amount of research can hope to capture and explain all its elements. It deals with the position of man versus the Cosmos, the mystery of life and death, the existence of the spirit. The mushroom is the catalyst that brings about the meeting between the microcosm and the macrocosm.

The Mazatec shamans have real and valuable knowledge which is to our benefit not to be lost forever.

Huautla.
Photo by Luis Miguel Ávila

1 - HUAUTLA, THE EAGLE´S LAIR

The first time I heard of the magic mushroom and the shamanic Ceremony was in a book by the distinguished professor Fernando Benitez, "The Hallucinogenic Mushrooms", which is part of a larger work called "The Indians of Mexico." The excellent book by professor Benitez developed my interest in Maria Sabina and her magic.

In 1972, I was an anthropology student in Mexico, when I decided to take a trip into the Mazatec Sierra. This was a radical change in my experience, seeing that was a direct confrontation with nature and all her barriers while I had all my life lived in Mexico City.

Teotitlan del Camino is the last village before beginning the climb into the sierra. The word Teotitlan in Nahuatl means "Land of the Gods". It was a very picturesque town in those days, and very hot. As soon as you entered the way to the sierra, all the known signs of civilization disappeared and the landscape became breathtaking. I always find language inappropriate to describe the beauty of the mountains.

After several hours of difficult climb, one could reach Huautla. It still is a town entirely of Mazatec Indians in the middle of the mountains in Oaxaca, even if now can be reached by a winding, two lane road. The name seemed to me to be descriptive of the town, since there are eagles living in the mountains, but also because it could apply to the spiritual ascension intrinsic to shamanic magic.

To behold the mountains themselves is a spiritual experience. You can find yourself when contemplating these mountains standing literally at cloud level totally removed from all worldly cares. The views that the mountain tops afford coupled with clouds and far off horizon at eye level in all directions is a humbling experience which paradoxically raises the consciousness too far off heights. To me the effect was like magic. I felt that the mountains were not empty but instead populated by spiritual beings which only had to be approached to find them, and that's the way it was.

That is when I realized that, in spite of social taboos, young people like me went to Huautla to find something holy, untouchable, God. There was a great mystery in the woods. Gigantic trees of great beauty. The silence punctuated with the singing of exotic birds. I used to find the Indian traps for catching small wild game, hidden from view so well that they appeared expertly woven into the vegetation. Suddenly, approaching clouds quickly cover the view and fill that air as if one were walking totally isolated from the land, the trees and the daylight; all falls silent and you feel as if you were into the clouds.

During my first visit, I did not meet any shamans, but I did find the magic mushroom, since the Indians freely offered them to me on the way.

The Mazatec Indians are brown, not very tall, and they laugh freely. I was struck by their vitality, even among the old people who you can find walking in the mountains. They are strong. On one occasion an Indian offered me a hut to stay in, and I accepted. His wife was with him, and she was carrying a large bundle of firewood. I offered to carry it for her, and she gave it to me with puzzled look and a smile. I regretted it as soon as I threw the bundle over my shoulder. It must have been about sixty pounds and the woman had carried without any sign of weariness going up and down the footpaths not missing a step, a feat that I could not duplicate. I had learned a lesson from this woman, even though I thought myself physically strong, and it made me feel pretty ridiculous.

We walked five or six kilometers over footpaths that were quite slippery and steep, from the "*Puente de Fierro*", or Iron Bridge, to Huautla. It took two hours but finally made it into town. Huautla reminded me of those village paintings by the Mexican painter Diego Rivera, with the colorful Indian costumes set off against their dark skin. There were plenty of palm hats and baskets, blue *rebozos* and colorful dresses. With flowers made by hand with uncanny skill.

Stone paved streets, and muddy paths, adobe houses, many dogs running loose; and a Catholic church from the Seventeenth Century next to the Plaza, giving one a sense of history. On the front wall of the primary school, there is a mural with the picture of Ricardo Flores Magon, a prisoner, writing tirelessly in his own cell. Underneath the picture is a reminder: "Ricardo Flores Magon was born here. He anticipated the Mexican revolution and died in his cell in the United States."

Everything in Huautla makes one think of Mexico's past. The people, the mountains and the landscape form an accurate picture of what Mexico is like in its most authentic form. Walking in the narrow streets and listening to the laughter of children as they talked in their own dialect, was an experience not unfamiliar to me, and I felt quite at home. The blue sky, the mountains and the flowers, all seemed alive to me with a vitality that I had not seen before.

The Mazatecs do not destroy their own habitat. It is their medium which serves their needs, and they leave it almost untouched in its natural beauty. I sat on a ledge that stretched as far as the eye could see. From here I could see the mountains and the impressive horizon of the sierra. In the nearby lowlands you can see the barely discernible human figures which moved around with agility and they reminded me of ants; I could imagine the old people with their full white hair and their incredible white clothes; the farmers walking with their utensils perched over their shoulders, barefooted women with their small children on their backs, wrapped tightly in their rebozos.

I considered them poor before I realized that I was judging them from my point of view, when in reality there were happy as they lived, amid the natural wealth of the mountains. The sun, sky, game, mountains, moon and nights full of stars, with their mysterious magic, can be seen without obstruction. Their gods, the lord and owners of the earth, are felt to protect them from harm and talk to them through their magic mushrooms. The city-dweller does not have the wealth of the poorest Mazatecs.

Suddenly, I felt that the city, with the smog and its subway, was hundreds of light years away. I was suspended in time. These villages have survived history, after five centuries of Spanish rule; no intruder had succeeded in changing their outlook, their way of life, their culture or their religious beliefs. The Catholic influence did not destroy the ancient rituals of the Mazatecs, it only changed them to accommodate the Christian ideals into the pantheon of Mazatec gods. In this place, tradition remains strong and I felt overcome by a sense of timelessness.

I felt the old Mexico live again as if the Spaniards had never laid claim to this territory. The ancient gods never lost their faithful. The shamans faithfully continued to cultivate the knowledge of their forebears. I felt a return to the Indian Mexico, to the true essence of this land, the one which existed before the conquest. Our Indian brothers, having become a little lost after the period of invasion and oppression, still nurture the spirit of the eagle warriors and the jaguar, who once danced in this lands to the beat of drums.

2- TEONANACATL, THE FLESH OF GOD

Teonanacatl is the name that Mexicas had for the sacred mushrooms in their language. It means literally: "The Flesh of God". After going through my fists experience with the mushrooms, I can well understand the name.

I was in a beautiful spot in the sierra near Huautla. I was between the Iron Bridge and the Baths (a waterfall). A beautiful river fed by the mountain rains flowed by.

I had with me several mushrooms that I had acquired from the Indians I met on the way, and I was looking for a solitary place. I wanted to have my fist trip by myself, in the middle of nature. I found a spot which was away from the footpaths and near the water.

That morning at seven, near the river, I ingested the sacred mushrooms for the first time. I sat in silence.

After about a half an hour, I noticed that the leaves began following me with their leaves and branches, as if they were having a conversation among themselves and looking at me. All the plants began to grab my attention as if by magnetic attraction. They oozed a powerful new energy which I had not associated with plants before.

I began to sense acutely all the movements of the plants, the rustle of leaves against the breeze took on gigantic proportions, every noise was clearly discernible no matter how slight the movement. I distinguished all the hues of green in a single leaf. The plants soon began to shout their presence at me, as if they wanted a conversation. I noticed them having a lively conversation and soon I joined them. We could both sense each other's presence.

Afterwards, I lost the sense of self. When I came back to myself, I had a terrible shock: I felt my body melting into the rocks of the spot where I was. I felt my body descend into the earth right through the layers of soil and into the kingdom of the Dead. All the associations with which I was familiar began to flow into my head: *Mictlan,* Hell.

I felt I was dead; I had become a skeleton and lay among the rocks. Shortly, my remains pulverized into ashes and the remaining physical presence disappeared into nothingness.

I forgot my physical self, there in the spiritual World of Nothingness.

Then I gained a bright consciousness. I was alone, solitary, and unbearable coldness invaded my backbone, it gradually invaded my entrails and my heart, it began to have an effect on my state of mind and my morale. I felt a great nostalgia and anguish, convinced that something totally unpredictable and terrible was about to happen.

I dozed off. I was far away from the reality of seven that morning, totally immersed in new realities which were disorienting in the extreme, going deeper and into the dark.

The sound of hundreds of insect woke me up from my revelry. But their noise was a cosmic cry. The sound of the crickets became a prolonged lament which filled me with terror and dragged me to the World of the Dead.

-What happened? Was I dead?
-My body. Where was my body?
-Did it still exist?
-Where was I? What was I?
I did not know.

I could see the river clearly. I could see Thought like water flowing through the banks. Though was Water in the Infinite River of Eternity.

I suddenly remembered the mushrooms. How long had it been? What had really happened to me? Where had my body gone?

I did not want to think of my dead. I wondered if this was really being dead. Soon I concluded that this was it.

I then felt the weight of age, of all the memories, carrying the through eternity. I lost sense of time.

Slowly, I began to felt differently, a birth.

Holy Christ! The excruciating pain on the Cross. I alternated between Birth and Dead, several times.

I was a dry collection of ashes. Even the last vestige of my bones, the skull pulverized shortly.

I began to feel away from the world where I was no longer physical being, where I was no longer man. I was now the plants, the river, and the sky.

I saw bright light cascading in golden waves, infinite variety of color and LIGHT.

Deep violet, bright red, brilliant green, serene blue. My ashes then disappeared and melted into the universe.

I was born again. Always forming and reforming in the Mother Womb.

From a little child, I became the Universe. I was the Universe proceeding in all directions at the speed of light, covering all beings, spaces, molecules, atoms.

Eternity. I knew that I was Christ and had died crucified.

I come back to Man. I can now contemplate the microcosm with all its myriad details until now unknown but always omnipresent. Thought is now multidimensional; I am no longer confined in three dimensional spaces.

I hear the tentative and faint voice of a small being explaining before Terrible Judge, both of them confined into a single Mind.

There is not escape. Mind is lost in the desert of the unknown, traversing bleak. Landscapes full of dark and deep abysses, where conscience dawns on ignorance.

To have lived so long in the belief that the physical being was all we were and to be thrust suddenly into infinite space was shocking, disorienting. To discover the Spirit within which was always there but never acknowledged, confined to this deep dark cavern somewhere within my being and illuminated solely by a spark of hope that someday I would acknowledge Him.

Death. Is Death the only Thing that holds Fear for man?

I sensed a great weight in my being as if gravity was exerting more force and discovered frailty in an old man. It is not physical Age but the Age of Eternity that weighs me down.

Physical matter has revolved around and around, dying and being born and re-born and re-born. Darkness. Pitch black. Light from an unknown source. Atoms, their presence multiplied gyrations. Every day the first atom is born and in the evening the last star is extinguished.

I am in the midst of all this happening with no particular sense of place. I sense that the Universe is eternal and the space is infinite.

What is man? A beginning or an end?

Every atom is a Universe. It all began when a Divine explosion occurred and set a chain reaction expanding from its original point to counter the Original Darkness.

I had never conceptualized the idea of an all encompassing Universe but now I had lived it. Man is an involuntary participant in the universe, guided by the instinct to search out the Light.

Every atom is indistinguishable from the essence of God. God is indistinguishable from the Universe.

Although dead, my thinking mind transcended it. I am two. The physical being is perishable. The spiritual is real, eternal. I sense a storm within.

The falling rain deafening thunder claps. The raindrops make terrible explosions as they hit the rocks and they fall interminably.

How long has it rained? I don´t know. Am I dead? I don´t know.

Again my body is encrusted on the rocks, thinly merged with the matter of the surface. I am now dizzy and the speed of the revolutions makes me smaller and smaller. The centrifugal force begins to crush what is left of my hard tissues. The noise is unbearable.

When my eyes open, my sight penetrates objects. Color, light, temperature are not concepts, they are objects. The noise is dead but the force continues to crush my consciousness.

I can feel my bones surrendering to a great weight. And when the incoming force disappears it turns into a great expansion of the physical Being. After having reached the space of a point I am effortlessly growing into limitless space.

My body now encompasses All: vegetation, rivers, oceans, continents and more. I do not know where it ends. Time and Space attain Cosmic proportions.

My eyes are no longer limited to three dimensions. Extraterrestrial noise is now invading my ears. All sensations are so disorienting that description is impossible.

What started out as tentative step into the unknown destination has now become fully exposed and fills me with strange and terrible sensations. My sight is filled with vistas of the past, millions and millions of years. A young man with the spirit of adventure sat down to eat sacred mushrooms and died. That was me. But in dying I returned to my telluric and cosmic beginnings from which no knowledge is provided except as one gradually attains it.

What started as a quest, an adventure has transcended the finite universe of my mind. Now I understood that the dead man was I. He had remained asleep in a deep cosmic dream, unperturbed in the Cosmic Womb. Warm, moist and far away.

I became God. A God who slept and dreamt that, millions of years lost in eternity, he had been a man. During my dream, the energy of Life invaded my being and made me feel like a man, not knowing if I was man or god.

Did I live, or did I dream that I lived?

Do not know. I am the dream of matter. I do not know if someday, any day, I will awaken. In the meantime, I dream of all the lives that have passed through my consciousness.

I am now an old god. Cosmic age is not like physical age.

In a fit of creativity, I become an embryo inside the Womb, a sleeping embryo.

But the Universe is also dreaming of itself. It dies every day and is reborn. My spirit sense the warm and pink matrix from which it will never exit. That matrix is called Eternity.

After the return follows the remembrance. It leads to an encounter with the real Me, the only I, shorn of artifice and cover, vulnerable and palpitating.

Return to the beginning of myself, to the root of being. You can see the clear color of infancy and childhood.

Suddenly a realization: I am not dead! I am truly alive! Repeating like a mantra, then with abandon. I was now at the edge of the river, as at the beginning, but this time the sun was setting in the horizon.

Afterwards there was time for the understanding to sink in that the world issues from its parents, the sun and the water, which populate the land with lush vegetation, such as Eden must have been.

After having trod through the world of Death I came to a world of Peace. Ecstasy came then.

The nostalgia of the lost Eden, finding the lost path of light that leads us back, return to the Christ and the Love of God.

I hear the voice of a little child and I am that child: Mama! Papa!

I still do not resign myself to losing the ideal and blessed state of childhood, wherein all is lit up with the Love of God.

The sun, the glorious afternoon, the woods, all is magic and mystery. It is an enchanted forest. The sun, the evening, the birds.

Golden light shimmers on the green leaves. The river sings, softly flowing along the bank, its murmur serving a background to the chirp of the birds in a symphony of worship of god.

It is an eternal sunset. A soft breeze touches my cheek and reminds me of the soft caress of my parents.

There is Nirvana, a balanced state of holiness, contemplation and light. The light of the first infancy, never forgotten; those days when I was closer to God than I knew.

God is in the river, the sun, the woods, the song birds, the sunset, in childhood, in the heart.

Why do we forget that in childhood we are closer to God? I then understood that we are all Adam, all Christ, and all part of God.

3 – IN EDEN AND IN HELL

I remember well that in one of the faces of my first incredible journey with the sacred mushrooms, I felt surrounded by skeletons and hissing serpents, which caused me to fear the unknown. Also I remember having seen the Horned devil standing before me, with a tail, just as we have come to know the familiar figure from religious lore.

What is surprising about all this to me is that I considered myself an atheist. Nevertheless felt that I was undergoing a purely religious experience.

I also entered Eden. There I was surrounded by birds and walked in incredibly beautiful forests. Any attempt to explain this experience in scientific terms is doomed to failure, because one cannot apprehend the meaning of these experiences at the intellectual level.

After I regained three dimensional consciousnesses I opened my eyes to the realization that I was still among the living. This filled me with a grateful happiness.

What had happened to me was beyond belief. Something that escaped my ability to understand.

In one single event, I had been dead, In Hell, had returned to a fetal state and been reborn, has dissolved into nothingness and entered a blessed state in Eden.

I had gone through a gamut of emotions, from abject fear to contemplation, to a blessed ecstasy.

Only one who has experienced similar experiences could appreciate all the depth of my experiences that day.

I died and went to that blessed mansion of Heaven and returned to this plane.

"I am not dead" I am really alive. Thank you Dear Lord."

What we are dealing with in these instances are not hallucinations, imaginings. On the contrary, it is a journey with faculties of clairvoyance, made possible by a projection of the soul into the astral plane.

From then on, I became an avid student open to Magical, religious and extrasensory interpretations of events in life. Things that I had not been able to rationalize before acquired nevertheless a solid shape before my eyes and to lose the one dimensional quality of fantasy began to feel that an internal order within which one can see several levels of existence interrelated among themselves which make it possible to apprehend other realities which exceed the capacity of the five physical senses.

The sacred elements in our lives are only apprehended by the Spirit, a part of our being which relates to the infinite and the eternal.

This experience and others that followed helped me to understand that Western civilization lives in the state of illusion supported by a science which is mostly atheistic in character and which is leading its citizen to destruction.

The ancient religions found the truth and they contain the true knowledge.

For instance, the Tibetan Book of the Dead is a guide to a holy death; it is a map so that the soul is not lost in the Abyss. After studying this book and others like it where the soul is accorded a place of honor and importance after death I was reminded of my experiences with the sacred mushrooms.

Magic is a real thing, something concrete and true which becomes credible only when the mind is ready.

My mistake on that first day was to take the mushrooms with neither guide not protection. I needed a Shaman who could lead me into the world of the Spirit. This would have avoided my feeling so lost and alone, hardly understanding the extraordinary worlds before me.

I fell into chasm. I faced directly the great mysteries of Life and Death from which we are protected in our daily lives lest it consume us, and I paid the consequences of my daring.

Without a guide, the Spirit is lost in the infinite space.

I hardly regret it, since it still was unique experience, one that cannot be repeated, only recalled.

I am one of the few mortals who have been able to see the world after death. This is a privilege and a great responsibility.

How could this be permitted to happen to me? I did not have the answer and I am still finding out. But was a great and terrible test which served to strengthen my Spirit and to open my consciousness to the higher worlds.

My life changed drastically. A great revolution occurred within which led me to the conclusion that my Self left my physical body, and traveled through the Astral plane, in the worlds that Magic and religion find in common.

After all these years I still am not fully certain why I was permitted to enter these worlds and to return. I hope that someone can profit from my experience.

I am a living being who walked among the Dead...

This concept is difficult to accept and understand fully. We are ready to accept only those things that we can apprehend directly ourselves. But to explore the unknown it is necessary to have courage. It is so easy to become a prisoner of fear.

Months later, I returned to Huautla motivated to find out the journey that I had experienced, and to make the acquaintance of Maria Sabina and her Ceremony.

Two friends came with me. We found a hut where we could stay. The owner was a man named Loreto, about thirty years old, married with four children. It rained very heavily that afternoon. The adobe hut had a carton roof and was very humble. The lady of the house offered us coffee which we drank gratefully, while she and her husband carried on a conversation in their dialect.

There was a picture of the Sacred Heart of Jesus on the wall. It was the only decoration. After we made ourselves at home, Loreto offered us the sacred mushrooms as a gesture of hospitality. They were covered in a banana leaf. We ate them, five for each, of the type called "*derrumbe*" by the locals. These mushrooms are not very large.

After some thirty minutes, I had a sensation of dizziness. Loreto put out the candles and the family went to sleep.

My friends and I were sitting on the floor in the middle of the room. One of my friends lit a cigarette and the light from the match blinded me with bright colors.

The butt of the cigarette was an intense light, like a miniature sun, that made a strange trajectory in the air, leaving a path of light where it had gone.

After a while, I do not know how long since I had lost the sense of time. I saw the hut filling with serpents. Their hissing became louder and louder. There were skulls on the floor. Once again, I felt myself fully transported to Hell...

This time I tried to observe objectively and without fear but without success. Someone lit a candle and I felt that when the candle burned out so would my life. The flame to me represented the Life of my body. Although I was greatly afraid, I tried to overcome the sensation.

Suddenly, the face of one of my friends become Death, a supernatural being, who was waiting for the candle to burn out before taking me away to this world. I lost my concentration and fell deeper into fear.

I raised my eyes and my sight fell on the picture of Jesus, a face that evoked peace and tranquility. The sight of Jesus was sufficient to help me overcome my fear and to vanish the serpents and death from the room.

I began to hear at that moment a sweet song somewhere in the distance. It had a twinge of sadness to its melody. It was the voice of a woman in another hut. I went out to see where the voice was coming from.

I understood. It was a Mazatec singing in her native tongue. Very likely she was also involved in a Ceremony, a *"Velada"*. I sat down outside our hut and listened in ecstasy the beautiful songs which filled me with peace. All the ugly and malefic figures disappeared from my presence. And I became filled with a sense of tranquility. It was so subtle and beautiful.

I felt as a special guest to that *Velada*. She had done a great good to me without knowing.

That night my "atheism" was greatly shaken. It was like a tower about to fall…

4 – MARIA SABINA

The next day I asked in town for Maria Sabina. A boy who heard me offered to take me to her.

-Do you want to go with Maria Sabina? I can take you to her.

-Please.

We agreed to meet at five in the afternoon.

My friends remained in Loreto's hut. I wanted to meet Maria Sabina, and intrigued by her already growing legend, I had decided to meet her one on one.

I had brought her a present: two oil paintings, of Christ and one a portrait of her that I had painting myself.

On the way, it began to rain in torrents. The boy German, -my guide- told me that the climb there takes more than one hour. The place was called El Fortin, and it was at the peak of the mountain.

We arrived there cold, tired and fully covered with mud. German knocked on the door. A young woman opened it and German explained to her in Mazatec the reason for our visit. She let us into the adobe house.

Inside it was peaceful and mystical like a church. None of the tempest seemed to intrude into the sanctuary. She was there. An old woman, white hair with gray patches, thin, not very tall, brown, Indian appearance. She was the famous Maria Sabina.

I suddenly realized that I was before one of the most famous healers on the face of the Earth. She had received many scientists who had come to study her telepathic and healing powers.

With reverence I Kissed her hand. She represented the highest attainment that I could relate to at that time. I gave her the paintings of Jesus and her own portrait. It was the first time I saw her smile. She led us into the kitchen and offered us coffee.

I dried my clothes over the fire and regained my spirit with the warm coffee, while we waited for the sun to set. The Ceremony of the sacred mushrooms is always done at night.

My guide and interpreter German had already explained that I came hoping to have a Ceremony. The young woman had already put all the necessary elements together.

Around nine o'clock, we went into the central room of the house. Maria Sabina ordered the figures on her altar: a figure of Jesus Christ, one of Saint Anthony, flowers, candles, and a brazier for the copal (Indian incense).

From a bag she took out several mushrooms, with a white stem and a dark bulb, the ones called *"derrumbe"* in Spanish, *"Di shi to"* in Mazatec.

They were medium sized, very dark. She gave me six and took six for herself.

She rubbed ground tobacco on my arms. This is called San Pedro and its function is to protect the tripper.

Maria Sabina lit the copal and passed the mushrooms several times over the smoky aroma while praying in a low voice. I felt filled with mystery and expectation, something solemn and sacred was about to happen.

German was my interpreter since Maria Sabina did not speak one word of Spanish. She signaled to me begin eating the mushrooms and we both ate together, in silence.

She chewed her mushrooms very slowly while I tried to do the same.

-Maria Sabina says to let her know when you begin to sense the effect of the mushrooms –German said.

Within thirty minutes I was feeling dizzy and I told her so. The taste of the mushrooms is very strong and stays with you for hours.

Maria Sabina put out the candles and sat next to me. She began to pray very low in Mazatec. She asked me my name and I told her.

She then began to sing also in a very low voice.

I saw many colored lights which changed in brightness and intensity with the tone of her singing. The singing was rhythmic and hypnotic. It was a shamanic chant, sacred, ancient. I felt her singing gently rocking me and transporting me to far away worlds.

Not once did I see terrible visions nor sense any other negative vibration. Instead I experienced infinite peace, the sensation of flying in a spiral of color. In the center of the room next to the wall, I saw a white light of great intensity. I asked German what it meant and he asked Maria Sabina who said that it was the Light of the Holy Spirit.

It was very impressive to me, that great white light.

It started to fade until disappeared completely from the room.

I lost consciousness of the room. I suddenly found myself in a flower garden, with fountains and birds flying all around, dense and beautiful forests. The Garden of Eden.

Maria continued to pray. Suddenly I heard Maria Sabina's voice:

-Saint Peter, Saint Paul, Lord Jesus Christ…
-Enrique, Enrique, Enrique, holy, holy, holy…

These words touched me very deeply and I felt like Jesus on the Cross. I could feel the Crown of Thorns; I could feel the blood dripping from my forehead. The light became visible again.

With the excuse that I was going to urinate, I asked permission to go out of the house, and I did.

When I was outside, I felt a great fear and the need to pray for protection....

I turned my face to the sky and saw the millions of stars and galaxies. I repeated the Lord's Prayer:

Our father, who art in Heaven
Hallowed by Thy Name
Thy kingdom come
Thy Will be done on Earth
As it is in Heaven.
Give us this day our daily bread
And forgive us our trespasses
As we forgive those who have trespassed against us.
And let us not fall into temptation
But deliver us from evil
For thine is the kingdom and the Power and the Glory
Forever and ever.

Amen

I recited the prayer with my eyes closed, and miraculously, the fear passed. I learned that the words to the Lord's Prayer hold a great power that puts the supplicant in touch with the Sacred Being.

I opened my eyes and looked at the sky. The stars made the shape of a face, a timeless visage, as of an old man with a long flowing beard and white long hair. I felt that this was the face of God in a human form, so I could relate to Him.

My body shook in ecstasy as I prayed for forgiveness of all my sins; I saw my life and my death pale in importance compared to the greatness that I was witnessing. A great interior peace took over me, and I had the sensation of power and balance, beauty and harmony.

I returned inside the house and sat next to Maria. Her quiet demeanor sitting there on the *petate* -the thin palm blanket- wrapped in her *rebozo,* without moving in her serene state, brought to mind the *gurus* of India sitting in an *asana*. She was all sweetness and serene, and powerful at the same time. We remained sitting there quietly, with only a candle to light the room. And she began to sing in a low voice again.

She stopped her song suddenly, and she smiled at me with a great goodness. I was totally impressed by the personality of this woman and her Ceremony. I was the High Priestess of the sacred mushrooms, who had been the subject of so many studies of scientists. I remember Benitez and Wasson, and I suddenly understood their description of the majesty and beauty of the mystic Ceremony of Maria Sabina. I knew that it was a privilege to be there and to hear her wonderful song.

She was all mysticism and wisdom, while her attitude was full of humility, although she was the High Priestess.

She put out the candle and began to sing again. Her singing permeated the night, enfolding me in light and cosmic images.

The lights multiplied and strengthened. I had visions of ancient Aztec and Mayan temples and palaces.

When the day dawned, I was asleep full of images without equal.

The next day, with German translating, Maria told me that she had seen my life. She had seen my parents, my house, my paintings, my books. She described the house where I lived and my parents.

-Maria Sabina says that your parents are older people, with white hair. She says you have many paintings of the saints, your mother has many stone figures and your father has many books...

She described things that she had not seen! I asked her how she did it, how she could see things that I had not described for her and that only I knew.

-She says that when she sings, she can see the lives of the people that come to her, their house, their health and their cure.

To me this was purely unbelievable. The extraordinary experience of the night before and now demonstrating that she had powers of telepathy and clairvoyance.

My regard for her increased tremendously that day. After taking photographs of her, I thanked her and said good bye. I returned to town. While this happened in 1972, I still remember it had been yesterday.

I continued to visit her and each time I took bread and cigarettes. The bread she gave to her many grandchildren and the cigarettes she kept for herself.

I returned to Mexico City. After several months, that night was still fresh in my mind.

The next time I returned to see Maria Sabina, it was with my parents. My mother was a dance teacher; my father was a lawyer and philosopher. Both wanted to meet her, curious about my experience with the sacred mushrooms. This time, the events in the ceremony were similar to what I had experienced previously, but she also took my mother by the arm and told her:

-Your left arm is very cold. You have a heart ailment.

I knew this to be true. My mother had undergone a cardiac problem some years before. I was baffled that without the benefit of X-ray nor any other aid she had diagnosed accurately my mother's condition. She had accomplished this with payer and song.

I did not know of any doctor who could do the same.

Nevertheless, I heard some medical doctors' remark in Mexico City that she was a charlatan and a witch. They could not accept that this humble woman had a secret knowledge that surpassed the scientific facts. I hope that someday she will find a proper place in people's consciousness, heir to timeless knowledge which surpasses our own understanding.

In this materialistic civilization we have learned to underrate the wisdom of Maria Sabina, we have lost any notion of sacredness; we have sacrificed the most precious spiritual treasures in exchange for materialistic well being. The atheistic science has brought man to the brink of destruction, with nuclear arsenals and merciless wars.

It is sad that the truly wise must live away from those who need them most, from those who live under the thumb of the destructive power of civilization.

The day man forgot God, and pretended to replace Him in the Universe; Man lost his way and Himself. It is a world of the blind leading the blind and falling into the abyss.

I still remember the afternoon that I went to say hello. I had a terrible pain in my bowel, and I told her. Maria Sabina put her hand over my stomach and prayed in silence. I felt her hand very hot. In five minutes, the area had become numb and the pain had disappeared! She lifted her hand and I thanked her. I still do not understand how she did it. I asked several doctors and all of them said it was autosuggestion. It seems incredible to me that they should try to explain a spiritual healing as something imaginary. Their explanation seemed incomplete to me.

Is there a doctor who could produce a diagnosis without the aid of technology, lab tests and instruments? Few of them. What doctors could look into the past of their patients and relate their illnesses to their actions? None.

Maria Sabina is an example of the power of the mind in the Mazatec shamans. Her powers have been the subject of serious studies in the United States and Europe, leading to controversy about the true nature of her powers. All those who have studied her, agree that Maria Sabina has something significant to offer and amenable to scientific study.

It has been more than a few scientists who went to meet her and study her healing powers, who went away unconvinced of her genuineness.

Since then, I stand in awe of Maria Sabina and what she stands for. I feel it was a great privilege to have known her and to have participated in her ceremony of the sacred mushrooms.

5 - THE GNOME

In 1974, I returned to Huautla. My previous experiences with the sacred mushrooms, and especially with Maria Sabina, had remained with me throughout the years. I had found new outlets to express my new consciousness, painting and writing. Those experiences had served to alter my consciousness about the world which surrounds me. I had begun to research by myself all the literature related to occult matters, looking for a meaningful interpretation of my experiences.

Everything that I had previously ignored became my most treasured findings. I always found something in each book that related to my experiences.

After checking into a hotel, I slept soundly to rest from the arduous climb into the mountains.

Next day, I found some mushrooms and took them that night in my hotel room.

At first I felt like a prisoner in the room. I felt the need to go into the mountains.

Suddenly, I decided to go into the night to Maria Sabina's house.

Without thinking of the lateness of the hour, I went outside and began walking out of town.

I got lost. Somewhere in the dark I had taken a wrong turn and continued to walk without finding the house. When I realized my predicament, I kept walking trying to find the correct way, but without success. By this time, I could see the town well below. I could tell from the dimness of the lights that I had walked too far.

Suddenly, the fog enveloped the place where I stood. The moon, the footpath, the foliage, all disappeared from view. Not knowing where to go, I stood there hoping for the fog to fade. I looked at my watch and it was almost midnight.

I felt a great aloneness. I was alone, in the middle of nowhere, lost and under the influence of the sacred mushrooms.

I decided to remain calm.

I felt better when the fog abated and the sky became visible. The moon now had an air of mystery.

I felt for the first time my aloneness before the Universe, the aloneness of my soul against Life and Death. We are born alone and die alone. At that moment, that realization hit me rather powerfully.

I lit a cigarette and suddenly a great happiness fell over me, and eternal peace.

The fog enveloped me again and the sky disappeared, but this time I had no apprehension. Instead, I felt pleasure and peace at the prospect of contemplating all around me at my leisure.

I was happy and calm.

All of a sudden, I was not alone any more. I say all of a sudden because there was no intrusion; it was apparition of a young man not more than twenty feet from me.

I did not see or hear anyone approaching; I saw no movement, only one moment he was not there and the next moment. He was.

I was surprised, but not afraid. I got very curious, and I walked over to where he sat.

He sat there, eyes closed, as if he were sleeping or in a trance.
I thought he must have eaten the mushrooms.

-Are you ok? Would you like a cigarette?

No response. I repeated myself, but he did not make any response.

His appearance confused me. I observed him closely. He had a shirt on, with knitted flowers on, and a pair of white cotton pants. He was brown, young. I remained next to him a while, smoking and observing him. I noticed that his presence was producing a strange sensation within me. It was a sensation that although I could see a body, it really was empty of all substance. There was nothing there. I felt nervous. His ears were pointed and when I noticed this, I stepped back with a jolt.

I strongly sensed that the being before me was not human.

His presence began to make me uncomfortable. I could feel that my own presence was not pleasant to him. I began to think that I was hallucinating. So I came closer to him only to discover that his ears were indeed pointed and that his physical appearance did not seem human.

I began to feel fear, uneasiness, and I turned around to get away from that place. I ran.

The legend of the gnomes in Mexico came to my mind. The ancient Mexican believed that non human beings roamed at night. They owned the night, that's why Indian life was confined to the day.

I looked at my watch. It was already one o'clock.

The Mazatecs talked about the mountain spirits who also live in the forest, the gods of Earth, and the children of *Chikon Nindo Tocosho*.

I naturally thought these were exaggerations, fanciful legends. They told me that the god's anger would kindle if one were disturb them.

This encounter was unforgettable to me.

The strangeness of this being and his silent intrusion into my space truly frightened me. I wanted to look back but did not dare. By this time the sky had cleared and I could see my way.

This time the lights of the town helped me to find my way. I went straight to Maria's house.

I knocked on the door. The young woman opened the door and let me in. Maria Sabina welcomed me. As best I could make signs that I needed to spend the night there. She understood and pointed out a *petate* where I could lie down for the night. Gratefully, I lay down and they turned out the light of the candle.

Within me, I was thanking God for my good fortune.

I felt protected, safe from danger, safe from that mysterious being that had appeared to me in the mountain.

6 – DON ERNESTO

My interest in the sacred mushrooms and its ceremony increased. I wanted to know more about the Mazatec shamans.

In 1976, I was a student of anthropology, and I had decided to return to the Mazatec sierra to get know some of the shamans.

I should however clarify that my mind was far away from the discipline of anthropology, since I did not share the same attitudes towards magic and religion that my fellow students had.

I was not interested in academic research, but in the search of the sacred and eternal. I was searching for the ancient approach which existed in pre-Hispanic times. I was not in tune with the materialistic attitude of most anthropologists, particularly those with Marxist bent.

I saw materialism as a prejudice, an obstacle to understanding the meaning of magic and religion. One needs a free and open mind to begin to understand the sacred themes.

Since that year, I have visited the sierra almost every year and I have met all the Mazatec shamans of the region around Huautla, with whom I have shared extraordinary experiences.

Among them was one in the town of San Isidro. His name was Don Ernesto.

He did not speak Spanish, and it was necessary to have an interpreter. There was a Mazatec woman who helped us in this regard. The objective of this Ceremonies was to heal people. In the instance that I am about to relate, it was a woman who was ill. We were in the same room with her, and Don Ernesto permitted me to view the Ceremony because of my friendship with the family.

He set a table where he had already placed the mushrooms, some candles, copal, maize seeds, and flowers.

Don Ernesto began the ceremony by lighting the brazier and burning copal. He blessed the mushrooms and gave some to the patient and then ate some himself. He began to pray in a hardly audible voice.

It was night time and the only light came from the candles on the table. He mixed the patient's name together with his prayers which were recited in a very low voice. After introducing the patient's name, he put out the candles and continued to pray but his voice became louder. As his voice increased in volume, his prayers became a rhythmic chant. After a while, he began to sing in his language.

The song lasted hours, varying in intensity and pitch, but not losing its rhythm. The song is also a form of prayer, but it can be slow and sad or happy and full of melody. Afterwards, Don Ernesto told me that the song helps him to "see" the ailment of the patient.

After two hours of a constant song, the patient began to raise her head from the bed and to show interest in her surroundings. Don Ernesto asked her family to pray together with him asking for the health of the patient. All began reciting the Lord's Prayer in a chorus.

As the prayers increased in intensity, the patient began to cry very emotionally.

Don Ernesto did not cease to sing and to burn copal the whole night. After several hours he dried his forehead which dripped with sweat constantly but did not lose a beat in his song.

I later found out that the prayer and the song is an exercise in concentration since it is not enough simply to vocalize the words. It is imperative to recite them with conviction and with intention. Prayer and song is the way to invoke the Powers and to concentrate them on the patient. Mechanical recitation is not enough.

The prayer and the song lasted all night so that by early morning the night had seemed to be rather tiring. Nevertheless, Don Ernesto did not lose his concentration the whole time. Finally, towards dawn, he stopped suddenly and began to talk with the owner of the house.

He revealed that he had seen the ailment and diagnosed it as an illness centered in the head of the patient. He asked for a hen, hen's eggs, and hummingbird feathers.

The lady promised to have what he asked for in the morning. The candles were lit once more and Don Ernesto ground some cacao beans, which he placed in a dish. He added water and spit the contents of the dish on the face of the patient. He sat once again at the table and began to sing.

When the morning light began to show outside; the lady entered with the things that Don Ernesto has asked for. He took the hen and very skillfully plucked out its heart and gave it to the patient to swallow with a glass of water.

He then used the maize seeds like dice and threw them on the table. After each time that he threw them, he studied very closely their positions and the direction in which they pointed. He predicted that the patient would recover.

They told me later that if the ends of the corn point towards the east that means that the patient will heal. If towards the north, it is a very bad sign.

He then took the eggs and placed them over the smoking fire, praying as he did so. He also took the feathers and together with the eggs wrapped them in maize leaves. He gave them to the patient and told her to bury them in her house, one bunch at the entrance, another in the center and the last one in a flower pot and to put the pot underneath the spot where she laid her head to sleep.

He told the patient that she had to abstain from sexual relations for five days in order not to interfere with the healing power of the Ceremony.

I could not ask Don Ernesto directly what I wanted to know. The owner of the house told me later that all had gone well, that the ailment had been caused by a malefic air that had entered the head. The death of the hen was a sacrifice for the life of the patient and the heart was a necessary element in the ceremony to strengthen the patient.

Don Ernesto drank some coffee in the morning and he seemed satisfied with the results. The patient was more active than the day before. Don Ernesto took leave of the family and returned to his town.

The song was one of the most interesting elements of the Ceremony. The act of sacrificing the hen for its heart was not entirely alien to me because I knew that pre-Hispanic Indians had similar practices. Even today, it is not unlikely that the Mazatec Indians still make sacrifices to ensure a good harvest. A turkey is slaughtered and its blood is sprinkled over the cultivated land to increase its fertility.

The maize was for me something new, but I have since confirmed that it is also a common practice among the Mazatecs for the purpose of divining and magic. North for the Mexica was *Mictlan,* -the region of the dead-. East related to the god *Quetzalcoatl.*

The shaman needs to commune with entities that reside in the spiritual world in order to get their cooperation to heal. The shaman must hold Death at bay, and ask God directly for the powers to heal. This was my introduction to the sacred mushrooms as a healing tool.

7 – PABLO

In September 1980, I went once again to Huautla in the sierra. I continued my interest in meeting shamans. I asked people of town. Pablo's name came up several times.
I found him in his wooden house, built at the edge of a mountain overlooking the abyss.
The view was impressive and beautiful from his house.

-Are you Pablo?

-At your service.

-I am looking for someone who can help me with a ceremony of the sacred mushrooms. I would like to know if you can do one for me, and how much you will charge me.

-Whatever you wish to give. I cannot put a price on it. It is sacred.
I was pleased with this response and demeanor. He was simple and direct although he seemed very poor. I was greatly touched by his selflessness.
We agreed to meet that night. He told me to bring the mushrooms, copal, candles, cacao, red hot pepper and holy water.
I arrived on time after sunset. It was beginning to get dark. I knocked on the door.
-Come in, the door is open.

I went in and gave him the things I had brought. While he did preparations I sat on the *petate*. We had a lively conversation in the meantime.
He lit the fire and began to burn the copal.

-Don Pablo, what is the difference between a healer and a *brujo*?

-Please don't call me Don, Pablo is ok. Think of me as your friend and talk to me with confidence. A healer is someone who knows how to heal the sick by working with the Divine being. The *brujo* is someone who works with the Devil to make others sick or to kill.

-What is a *nahual*, Pablo?

-They are brujos who change into animals or into devils.

-Do they really exist?

-Of course.

-And the healers, do they also change into something else?

-When the healer heals people, he becomes a god.

-Can you tell me something about the sacred mushrooms?

-Well, they are something wonderful. You can see very deep to resolve problems. When someone gets sick, their spirit ends lost somewhere out there. With the mushrooms, you can find their spirit, in the mountains, the gorges, the basements, the woods, and the bottom of the sea. Even in other planets or the Great Beyond.

-Pablo, the practice of eating the mushrooms is very old, is it not?

-Yes, very old, very ancient. Before the Spaniards came, the Mazatecs already had this tradition. I inherited my knowledge from my dead mother. She was a good healer.

While we talked, Pablo made the fire in the brazier. He had already arranged the candles on the hard packed earth floor and he had taken out a prayer book and a rosary. Before proceeding too far, he held the mushrooms over the smoky fire smelling of copal to bless them. We knelt before the candles, facing east, and he began to pray. He prayed for a very long time in a very low voice which was barely audible.

Later on he told me that the altar had to face the East because we had to face the rising sun.

After a long while, he gave me my mushrooms to eat and he took his. We both ate. He put out the candles and we remained silently in the dark for almost two hours.

The noises of the nighttime insects took on an unreal intensity. While observing silence, I began to recollect my life, as if I was watching a film. I felt an obstacle in my life which prevented me from realizing my most cherished goals. I made an analysis of my life errors, and tried to do it objectively as if I were reviewing some else's life.

I was suddenly overcome with the desire to lie down on the floor, face up. I felt myself being born!

Pablo said that I was reliving my birth and my life. Without prompting, Pablo began to mention events in my life which I had never told him in the few hours since we had met.

I should not have been surprised. Seeing that Maria Sabina had already something of the sort before with me and with my parents. But I was still awed by it all. This is a common feature of the Mazatec healers. They can look into your life and tell you about without being told anything about you. Some of it has to do with the transmission of the thought. I was thinking of my life. But I still did not know how he did it.

He told me that most of my problems were caused by envy.

-How can you know these things about my life?

-You are telling me with your mind. With the sacred mushrooms, I can see your past, your illnesses, or if you are the target of sorcery, *brujerias*.

-Sometimes I have horrible dreams. I see ugly devils and satanic things. Can you tell me how to put an end to these things?

He asked me a description of my dreams and began to throw up.

-Pablo, are you all right?

-I am helping you to vomit those malefic beings that are damaging your mind. You should vomit, but I did it for you. You have to destroy the books on Satanism and black magic that you are keeping in your house. That's why you have all those dreams…

I couldn't believe my ears. In my widening search for explanations on magic and the supernatural I had acquired some books on black magic.

-How do you know?

-I told you that I can see the life of people. It is a divine gift that comes to fruition with the mushrooms. You do not understand now, but in time you will.

-And are you saying that those books are causing my nightmares?

-Yes. And you have to destroy them, as soon as possible. Don't give them away and don't throw them away. Burn them. There is something you must learn. It has to do with the practice of the mushrooms.

-What practices?

-Listen well. After you commune with the mushrooms, you have to abstain from sexual relations for five days. This is very important. If you do not, then the work accomplishes nothing. Do you understand?

-All right. I will do it. But what relation is there between the mushrooms and sex?

-I must have seemed confused or disappointed because he began to laugh as if we were watching a total neophyte.

-What do you mean what is the relation between those two? Don't be a fool. Do not be confused. The mushrooms are divine and sex is the lowest. It is pure materialism. It is as if you decide to go into a church and to have sex. It is a profanation.

-Now I understand.

-Yes but understanding is not enough. You have to do it. You think too much of women. This keeps you from rising to higher worlds.

Pablo was right. I was constantly fighting between two ways: the spirituality and the sensuality. I told Pablo how amazed I was at his findings. I asked him if he was willing to teach me his knowledge.

-I can teach you, but you have to abide the rule of the five days. If you don´t. Then I have nothing to teach you.

In a few hours with Pablo I had learned a lot more about the occult knowledge and psychology from the magic mushrooms than with the university books. He had completely analyzed my life and told me what was keeping me from progressing, and I had not mentioned anything to him. That night he was my psychiatrist, my confessor and my friend, at the same time he became my teacher. I felt a great respect for him that in spite of his appearance of poverty and simple humility he was in reality a wise man. He was hidden in the mountains and knew more about me than myself.

-How did you learn this, Pablo?

-I learned it all from the mushrooms. Once in a trip I entered the trunk of the tree of wisdom, to its deepest level and I found all the answers. The Great Wise One asked me what sort of knowledge I desired and I said: -All- and She asked "Will your mind be ready?" I said: "I will try". And the Great Wise One gave this knowledge which is all buried deep in these lands.

We continued to talk until dawn. It was like two old friends and we fell asleep from tiredness. I felt a great liberation, completely relieved of all my sins and my material weight.

Next day we continued the conversation. I told him that I had studied Anthropology and that I have found those in the field to be completely taken over by materialism and Marxism. And that they refused to acknowledge the world of magic and the sacred element in all of us. He told me to forget about the scientists.

-They are more lost than the rest of us. They are sure that God does not exist. I saw those who came to confirm the reality of the mushrooms. This is something sacred and they could not see.

He was scornful of the scientists that he had seen.

-Huautla became lost when they arrived. They talked about the mushrooms to all and sundry. There was nothing they would stoop to. To the mushrooms was not an entity, it was a drug that makes your mind hallucinate. The mushrooms are something greater. You know it now. After a few months that the scientists had been in Huautla, a lot of tourists came here, gringos and hippies who did not know the meaning of respect.

I knew he was right, although I had never seen it from his point of view. The simple but sacred rite had become a tourist attraction, a sort of Mexican curios. People from all around the world had come, but none had been on the right Path. Huautla did not need these visitors who thought nothing of profaning the sacred worlds. Huautla did not need all those scientists who had come to debunk its ancient tradition. I had never seen it through the Mazatecs' eyes. To them the arrival of strange and exotic visitors who had not regard for the occult knowledge and skill conferred by the mushrooms was a disaster; it was social and spiritual pollution. The mushrooms had become a commodity with a price. Pablo continued:

-Those scientists did not take note of the sacred meaning of the mushrooms nor of its taboos. They completely ignored the rule of five days or the consequences. They could trip, but their destination was pure Hell.

I did not want to tell Pablo but at that moment I understood why my first experience had been so horrible. I myself had not known any of the things that Pablo was imparting to me. I had always observed the healers use copal in their rituals. Cacao was a universal element everywhere I had gone with the help of a healer.

-Pablo, what are the powers that the mushroom confers?

-In order to acquire those powers, it is necessary to understand the Path of your trip. You must have courage and you have to stand whatever your trip shows you. You can see many things without knowing what they are. Those who take the mushrooms for the first time suffer greatly. It is natural, just as it should be. All the pain from the past crowds the mind. But once you get over it, you are totally at peace. Many things become clear. You no longer have this anguish. I have always been able to confirm that the mushrooms are something wonderful. It takes you to the bottom of things. My forefathers, they were great priests, my mother was one.

-What prayer do you say?

-Once you smoke the mushrooms over the copal, you bless them seven times with the sign of the cross. You ask the spirits to make the mushrooms talk. If you are caught somewhere, in a bewitched place, the mushrooms goes to pick you up and bring you home. Home is your body. That is why you have to invoke the Mountains, the Earth, the Wind, Water and Fire, our gods. With their help, you can heal the sick. But to do this, you have to be clean and pure.

-What happens when the healer is not?

-He is not a healer.

-Then it must be very difficult to be a healer.

-It is.

Photo by Luis Miguel Ávila

8. THE MUSHROOMS CEREMONY

In this chapter, I am going to list all the necessary elements for a Ceremony. The objective is normally to heal a sick person from a physical or spiritual ailment. The ceremony is therefore a cleansing, an exorcism, and a communion with the most sacred.

FIRE, CHARCOAL AND COPAL

Fire is essential in the ceremony. It relates to the sacred fire in all the solar religions. The names of some solar gods are Christ, Krishna, Quetzalcoatl and Osiris.

It is important that the brazier always have a fire going since, otherwise the patient remains vulnerable to the attacks from malignant entities. To scare them away, copal is used. The resin from the trees has a great power to protect, although it is also possible to use incense with the same objective.

Copal is a substance which has been used in pre-Colombian times for use in religious ceremonies.

RED HOT PEPPER

The smoke from the red pepper is an irritant to the malignant beings who are attracted to the *Veladas* (Ceremonies). It is burned to expel devils and astral larvae.

RAW GARLIC

The garlic is chewed to return the patient to the earth plane from the astral plane. It is particularly necessary when the patient gets lost in the astral plane during a trip with the mushrooms.

CACAO

Cacao is spiritual gold, the only acceptable offering to the higher beings, namely the gods of Fire, Earth, Water and Air. The offering is the form of assimilation. One eats the cacao in order to become worthy to acquire the power of the mushrooms. It is to prevent the loss of reason as a result of the trip.

In his book, *"The Wonderful Mushroom Teonananacatl"*, Gordon Wasson says the following:

"The pre-Columbian aristocracy in America used to eat sacred mushrooms accompanied with cold chocolate mixed with maize and flowers *"Quaraibea funebris"*, which the Indians used to call *Poyomatli*. Mushrooms were never eaten with alcoholic beverages. Eaten the mushrooms squashed were more common in antiquity than it is today."

Cacao is a fit offer to the Earth God, who in Mazatec is called *Chicon Nangui,* and who according to legend is the master of hills and mountains. If an offer is not made, he can cause the trippers to suffer.

CANDLES FROM VIRGIN WAX

Some healers use thirteen candles. Unless made from virgin wax, the candles are not fit to be used. They are used to assist in prayer, an essential element before taking the mushrooms. The thirteen candles represent Christ and the Twelve. Although this is now a Christian symbol, the number thirteen was also sacred in Meso-America. Contemplation of the candles helps to develop clairvoyance.

HOLY WATER AND THE ROSARY

Holy water serves to cleanse the mushrooms and the participants. The cross is drawn on the forehead, the temples, and the chest. Another method to return someone from the astral plane is to throw holy water on the face and crying out the person's Christian name. The holy rosary is used to count the number of prayers during the Ceremony.

CHRISTIAN IMAGES

While the practice of using Christian images is not common to all healers, it is nevertheless true that all have incorporated Christian themes into their Ceremonies. Many prayers are said in Mazatec and relate to the Indian deities, but the tradition is now decidedly Christian.

It is possible however to profit from the Ceremony, no matter what religious context is followed to reach their own God speaks.

SACRED MUSHROOMS TEONANACATL

Teonanacatl means literally "Flesh of God". The mushrooms are the central element in the Ceremony, as it opens the window leading to the higher planes of consciousness.

The scientific name is *Psylocibe Cerulescens Mazatecorum Hein*. The Indians call it *"Derrumbe"* in Spanish, indicating that they tend to grow on edges of mountain gorges. In their language, they call it *Di Shi Too,* which means "things that burst forth."

The healer decides on the doses for each participant. It is believed that the mushroom is an entity that takes the participants to commune with God.

To be eaten the mushrooms must be purified, with smoke from the brazier, with prayer and with blessings. The cross must be drawn over them seven times. They are then held over the smoke of the fire and the copal.

HEN EGGS AND HUMMINGBIRD FEATHERS

The eggs must come from a ranch hen, meaning organically grown. They are utilized for cleansing the patient and to trap the ailments, or the evil influences. The feathers are offerings to the gods of the earth (Chicon Nangui) and of the water (Chicon Nanda).

MAIZE

Maize serves to make predictions. The corn seeds are thrown on a flat surface like dice and readings of where they are pointing are made by the healer. This will help foretell the outcome of the Ceremony. Use of the maize for this purpose like the rest of the Ceremony is very old.

RULES FOR A SUCCESFUL CEREMONY

The body must be clean before taking the mushrooms. This is accomplished mainly by fasting. The lightness resulting from fasting makes it easier to enter the astral plane.

The Ceremony must be at night. During the day you run the risk of interruption by the profane. The Mazatecs only do them at night. The darkness and the silence set the conditions for spiritual activity and clairvoyance. The Ceremony must be made inside the house, however, not outside.

Communion with the Flesh of God must be approached with humility and respect, but without fear. You should have a healer to assist you, or a person with experience in mushrooms. Fear is an obstacle in the Path, especially when you encounter the power of God.

The beginning of trips is always confusing and terrible, one must remain as calm as possible. After a while things become clearer and it is possible to reach the state of ecstasy. At first you must speak very little, a little as possible. Later you can talk as much as you desire at any time. Too much talk however loses concentration and energy.

Only the participants must be present. They must not be very much. The vibrations of too many people soil the atmosphere.

For your safety, you should not leave the protection of the house! Outside there are always evil spirits who will attack you. To defend against them, copal and cacao are a must.

They are a shield against evil.

You must never swear nor shout. Unnecessary noise is disruptive. The rule is to remain silent, concentrating on prayer, meditating deeply to open your mind to extrasensory impulses.

Sexual abstinence is also a must. However, you must observe it five days before and five days after the Ceremony. You may not eat pig meat during that period either. Healers observe these rules particularly in order to become worthy of healing others.

The Indians used to take a steam to cleanse the outside of the body. They did it before and after the Ceremony, to protect the body from cold caused by the mushrooms.

Some ceremonies are undertaken to ask for special favors from God. In exchange, the petitioner promises some sacrifice for a period of time, such as sexual abstinence. This is particularly popular when asking for the health of someone or for success in farming. No food may be dropped on the floor. The promises made at the Ceremony must be kept by all the participants.

Popular folklore attributes great miracles to these rituals. The solemn promises are to be observed rigorously.

9. THE GODS

There are four important gods: Earth, Water, Air and Fire. The Mazatec tradition has remained faithful to the worship of the four, who are held in high respect. They are living entities and worthy of gifts. They live in another dimension.

Thanks to them we are able to exist, since they provide to us all the necessities of life. However, they can cause us harm, illness even death. Most illnesses are caused by the gods of the Earth and of Water. They usually exact payment from individuals who have not respected them or who have misused their powers.

Chicon Nangui is the name applicable to the gods of the Earth. *Chicon Nanda* applies to the gods of Water. They are like children when they act mischievously. They are found in lonely places, hard to get places. They made themselves visible only when they wish to scare interlopers away.

They can hypnotize people or drive them insane. The *Chicon Nagui* is the best known. They steal the soul, leading the body to illness. The people of Huautla call them *gods* or *owners of the land*. There are many legends about them. The Mazatecs offer them many gifts to remain in good terms with them.

Cacao is the most popular gift. People also use hummingbird feathers, or *guacamaya* hen or turkey eggs.

The mountain near where Huautla is located is called "Mountain of Worship". It is believed that a god lives there and owns the place. The Mazatecs call him *Chicon Nindo Tocosho* in their language, which means "The Lord (Owner) of the Mountain." It also can be translated as The Fair-Haired One of the Mountain."

No person lives there. It is a sacred place. The healers climb to the shrine there to deposit their gifts and to burn copal. Some leave lit candles behind. The objective is not only to keep in good terms with the god, but also to gain power to heal others and to seek protection.

When Pablo explained these things to me, I told him about my encounter with the young man in the fog. He told me:

-You were lucky. That sort of encounter is dangerous. He could have killed you or made you insane. If you came out unhurt it is because you have a powerful spirit yourself. The gods hurt people only when they walk an evil path. You might be vulnerable if you have already caused harm to another human being or to Nature.

-Can you protect yourself from them?

-You could dig into the ground with a knife seven times, or you could piss on the ground. That will make him disappear. The best protection however is to be pure, clean without blemish. Do not harm to others, to animals or to Nature. Leave everything in Nature the way you find it.

-How can you avoid this?

-You have to. Do not destroy anything nor sully places where you have been. Making disturbing noise, making unneeded fires, destroying trees, all this disturbs the gods in their places and they come back at to you. Strong winds or rains are caused to scare you away. If not, the insects can attack you and make you uncomfortable. The insects are messengers from the gods. On the other hand, if you walk with respect for nature, nothing will disturb you. Hunting now is a very bad thing. All the places in the mountains and the woods have their own gods, the real owners, and they are invisible.

Pablo continues:

-If you build a house, take care to make an offer to the gods of the place first. Ask for permission to use the land, the water, the trees, all the elements. If you do not, then you will surely fall ill. If you drink the water, you will find that it makes you sick. If on the other hand, you follow the simple rule, then they will sustain and prosper you. Once I saw the gods of Water playing like children in a river. I was walking near the river where no one lived. It was midnight, and I thought: "Children playing at this hour? Is this normal?"

-That's when I understood that it was not children. I could hear their laughter, their voices, loud and without fear. I was totally absorbed with wonderment. They could walk on the water and cross the whole breath of the river. I could not cross it swimming because the current was to strong. They walked effortlessly over it.

-Could anybody else have seen them, if they were with you?

-Of course not. If there had been someone else with me, it more likely that we would not have seen a thing. These visions are only visible to those who are clean, and in solitary places. They live in the rivers, the woods, the caves, the untraveled mountains. The places untouched by man that is where you can find them. Those must be in enchanted places.

10. COMMUNION WITH THE SPIRITS

Pablo said once:

-Humans do not die. We simply leave one body and pass into another plane of existence.

After his explanations, I know that we go to another dimension. To our consciousness, life after death is as real as life on the physical plane, but by comparison it is more subtle, because it is less heavy.

The spirits of the dead are invisible to our senses but they can communicate with us mentally, telepathically, with instances of telekinesis.

The first time that I felt the presence of a spirit was in Huautla. I was tripping with the sacred mushrooms.

There was a student friend of mine who had attended high school with me. He was also a teacher on Logic. We had similar social and political ideals. Those were the days of revolutionary activism, around the end of the sixties beginning of the seventies. My friend died of his wounds contracted in June of 1972 in Mexico City. Many students around the School of Education died that month.

His name was Francisco Trevino. He was very intelligent and I had a great regard for him. His dead was a shock to me, and I will always remember him.

Years later he stood with me in a Ceremony when I was under the influence of the sacred mushrooms, and we had a conversation telepathically.

His face took shape in a tree trunk. I saw his face distinctly on the bark of the tree. It was nighttime and I was in the wood.

His likeness remained young; his eyes full of hope and enthusiasm, his lenses made him look the intellectual. He told me not to feel sad for him, that he had not died. He said that he was living in another dimension and that the ideals for which he died would someday become reality for all. His face disappeared and the rest of his body faded away.

I had other experiences afterwards, where I could feel the presence of other persons whom I knew had passed away.

Months later, I was in Mexico City in a Ceremony of my own, and I thought of my grandmother on my mother's side. She had been very good to me before she passed away when I was a child. At that time, I had very strong emotions about her. Suddenly, the frame of her picture creaked, the noise extended to the door and the wall. I remained calm in spite of my fears and tried to understand the meaning of the event. Other instances came to my mind when the rooms had creaked rather loudly and I decided to pray.

The After Life…This is a great mystery for all of humanity. All the religions claim that our life does not end here. The experiences I had with my grandmother's spirit raised my consciousness about the subject. Ever since my first experiences with the sacred mushrooms, I experienced the spiritual essence of our being. I felt the conviction that the spirit is immortal, eternal, that it is the true self which uses the physical body in successive lives to evolve its consciousness. This realization only came to me through my communion with Teonanacatl.

Months later with Pablo, my father's spirit revealed itself to me. We were sitting in the dark. Pablo began to talk in a low voice, as if he were talking in secret with someone. I thought he was talking to me but soon realized that he was talking to another person. He seemed to be listening and then responded.

When he finished the conversation he told me that my father was saddened by the fact that I forgotten his library and that it was full of dust and forgotten. It had been his favorite room and I had felt a great loss when he passed away. I could not bring myself to enter the room, and therefore the neglect.

I had never mentioned to Pablo anything about my father's library. I noticed that when Pablo spike with my father there was the silhouette of a man in the dark with us. But I was afraid and did not look directly at the place where it was.

When I said that to Pablo, he said:

-You should have looked. Fear is a great obstacle in the trips with mushrooms.

-Pablo, did you really talk with my father? It is possible to talk with the dead?

-Of course. People do not die; they simply go to another world. There we have to give a full account of our actions in this world. Once I spoke with Juarez, afterwards with Cuauhtemoc and Cuitlahuac. They are invisible, but you can hear their voices. The mushrooms have taught me that the dead really live in another dimension.

That day I understood my first experience when I walked among the Dead, when I felt dead and my body reduced to ashes, and still fully conscious. I mentioned it to Pablo and asked him what it meant.

-Did you pass the threshold?

-I died and rose again.

-Then you went Beyond and returned to this world. The mushrooms gave you permission to know the next world before dying. You are very fortunate to have gone beyond in your fist trip. It took me a long time to accomplish it.

-You have too?

-Many times. The first time I laughed all the way through.
-Why laugh?

-Well, you are not a healer and therefore do not know anything about the Great Beyond. I know what you felt. I have passed through that many times, so I am no longer afraid.

Sometime later when I was alone in the house, my father came close to me. I was in my study, in silence. The glass panes began to make noise as if someone were hitting them. I looked but no one was there. I sense a call from my father to go to his library.

I steeled myself and went there. When I entered, I felt his presence as if he were sitting at his desk. I said the Lord´s Prayer and greeted my father.

-Father, how are you? I know that you are here. I want you know that I miss you very much, and from here I send you all my love...

I remained in the library a while with my father, I lit a candle and left the room. I did not hear the glass panes make any more noise that night.

A more dramatic event occurred years later. This time I was in the mountains near to Pablo's house. I was alone watching the stars. In the Sierra they look absolutely beautiful. My mother had passed away one year before and I always remembered her with love and sadness.

After a few hours under the stars, I left my physical consciousness. I saw a silhouette in the distance walking on the mountain, with the horizon and the stars as a backdrop. The figure was coming towards me and it was a woman wearing a white *rebozo*. There was an air of sadness about her. As she came nearer, I recognized her. She was my mother!

She resembled a peasant woman, but looked like a mystic. Her face reflected sadness and when she approached me she disappeared completely. I am sure it was she...

-Mama, how are you? I want you to know that wherever you are my heart blesses you.

I was then able to control my perception. If I closed my eyes, I could see a strange world in another dimension, with strange beings surrounding me. If I opened them I could see my physical surroundings in the mountains, the stars above me. With a simple action I could change my place: the Great Beyond or the here and now.

My mother's image became embedded in my memory. The sacred mushrooms had taught me a lesson, that we are spiritual beings with Immortal Life.

11. NAHUALISM

My interest in the occult and Indian magic led me to research other books on the subject. I read avidly the books published by Carlos Castaneda. I found many interesting things there. Also found similarities between his experiences and mine. Nevertheless, many of the things related by Castaneda seemed sinister to me, and awoke serious doubts about the objectives of Nahualism.

I spoke with Pablo about the books on don Juan.

He told me that he had heard about them, mainly from hippies. He had not read any, but he has not interested in knowing more about them because he was against nahualism. He said:

-Don Juan is a *brujo*. He is a *nahual*, right? Well, *nahualism* is part of black magic. These things about changing into an animal are diabolical. It is a filthy act not fit for humans.

Men have a spirit which is much more evolved than any animal.

Nahualism is a step backwards for the spirit. We the healers oppose the *nahuales*; we know how to heal, to raise the spirit of those who suffer and to return it to its rightful place. The people call as "avocats" or intermediaries because we intercede for the souls of the sick and the sinners before the Divine Justice. The *nahuales* use their power to kill; they ally themselves with the Devil and Death. They change into animal forms. To me there is not interest in learning how to change into filth.

I was frankly surprised by what he told me. I Found logic to it and tried to explain to him the elements that Castaneda expound on.

-I still think that you are talking about diabolical things. The "allies" are demons who can turn someone into a very powerful being, but in exchange for their spirit. The publicity on nahualism had led many to lose their way. Black magic is a trip without return and it leads to destruction. My knowledge as a healer is a higher learning. You are better off learning to heal like I do, than to delve into nahualism.

-Are there any nahuales in the Sierra Mazateca?

-Of course. They change into devils to make people sick or to kill. They can change into snakes, coyotes, birds or prey. The nahual women change into hens, she-turkeys or vultures. They usually live in faraway places, although you can find some in the villages. They live hypocritically not letting on what they are. During the day they look and act normal, but at night they change. I can always recognize the nahuales.

-How?

-By their gaze. They have a lost gaze but they look aggressive and fixed, like a bird or a prey. They emit bad vibrations, they are dark. They seem sick, pale, they eyes are dark. I always find it easy to recognize them.

-How can you defend yourself against a nahual?

-You turn the earth seven times with the point of a knife, and if you do not have time, then you piss on them. That is how you nullify their advance.

-Let me tell you something that happened to me outside Huautla one night. I had eaten mushrooms, and I was towards the landing to trip. It was about midnight and I was alone. In the dark I noticed a man squatting at the edge of the path. I thought that maybe he was defecating but I also thought it was strange that he had picked such a public place. As I passed him, I smelled a very strong odor of skunk which disappeared as I walked away. Could this man be a nahual?

-Surely. The odor is the sign of the nahual when they do not mean any good. He probably only wanted you to leave the place. If you had pissed right there, he would have left. This sort of encounter is dangerous, but if you know what to do, nothing happens. For instance, I can walk anywhere at any time and I never meet up with anything untoward. But before, I certainly did. When I was younger I used to tempt my luck. I used to go out at night to solitary places, but I had the power to do it. There was a place that nobody liked to pass because they feared it. They said that it was a malignant place. I went there one night, and when I got there my horse refused to obey me, as if someone else was holding him. I could only see the trees and the vegetation. Between the trees I could see a pair of glowing eyes which were fixed on me. I know all the animals in the forest and I can tell you that this was not one of them. Instead of letting fear take hold of me, I took my gun and shot in the dark. My horse, which seemed to be hypnotized, suddenly sprang to life and galloped away from that place. This was foolhardy and there are many who style themselves to be courageous. You do not know the meaning of courage until you are alone. There are places which are inhabited by dark spirits. You have to be prepared to cross them without incident.

12. PHILOSOPHY, PSYCHOLOGY AND TELEPATHY

The knowledge of the healers could be reduced to those three words. This knowledge which has been passed from ancient times is also religion and magic.

Telepathy is the transmission of messages only with thought. This is an integral part of the ceremony, between patient and healer. Several healers showed me that they knew what I was thinking, including incidents from my past that I had never discussed with them. This was a demonstration that the patient cannot hide anything from the healer: his soul, his past or his present.

They use of Psychology to find out about the character of the patient. They discover his traumas, his childhood, which are brought out by the mushrooms. The same thing happens with weaknesses and faults. The sacred mushrooms also provide the answer regarding how to overcome them. A good healer must be a good psychiatrist, has to be able to go deep into the psyche of the patient. Some try to hide the truth, but they are exposed during the ceremony.

One may have to go finding a soul deep into hell, but it cannot hide. With the sacred mushrooms, one can discover thieves, killers, or any other secret in one's life. Sooner or later all come out either by confessing, acknowledging, or revealing their acts, secrets, fears and all. When these secrets are evil, they usually represent a reluctance to face one's conscience.
With Teonanacatl, all your misdeeds are brought to light and you cannot avoid it. It is like the Final Judgment, the judgment of the soul. It is also the agent of Truth.

The patient confesses everything to the healer who in turn can do so much for him when the confession is voluntary and sincere. When the patient does not wish to confess, his suffering is beyond belief. The suffering is ended when the mushrooms leads him to confess.
The ceremony with Teonanacatl is a spiritual and emotional catharsis. The patient must vomit all his sins because it is the only way.
The philosophy imparted by the mushrooms is real and wonderful, it is unique, and it is direct knowledge of sacred things that you are going to learn in any university. Through Teonanacatl, we learn self-knowledge and our place in the Eternal and Infinite Universe.

Through the sacred mushrooms we learn about the universe within, we can travel beyond our physical life and death, we can transcend the conventional limitations of our little minds and come face to face with the Grand Visage.

The powers conferred by Teonanacatl are also magical; they lead mastery of clairvoyance and telekinesis. I have witnessed instances of clairvoyance from the healers who knew nothing about me. Magic is another dimension since when you master the powers of the mushrooms you also work with the internal energy of the Elementals. They cure through the transmutation of the patient's energy.

I have also witnessed incidents of telekinesis. I have seen charcoal burst into flames without anyone lighting a match. I have seen objects illuminated with light from the face of the healer.

In one instance with Pablo, the brazier moved by itself about three and a half feet without anyone touching it. I was told of another instance when a guitar flew across the room.

It is fair to say that what one psychoanalyst might achieve with a patient in weeks or months of work with him, it could be achieved in one night with the mushrooms. The analyst must coax the patient to speak about himself while the healers break through all the barriers of self-protection of the patient simply because the mushrooms will not tolerate dawdling. I know of some analysts who have begun to use the mushrooms in their sessions, although they are not fully convinced of its sacred character.

To be able to direct the powers of the sacred mushrooms, it is important to be clean and pure. People who ignore the sacred mysteries are not likely candidates for this stern discipline. They are full of bad karma and lead sexually disorganized lives. This is the major obstacle to acquiring the powers of Teonanacatl. In other words, being soiled in mind and soul, they enter the world of the mushrooms in a profane manner.

Those who do not understand will surely feel the urge to criticize or attack me, but the power of the mushrooms is stronger than they. Many will reject these ideas, particularly because of the commercialization of the mushrooms that has occurred. But this is not the only casualty, the Night of the Dead among the Purepechas (an indigenous group from Michoacan Mexico), and the ceremonies of Peyotl among the Huichol, have suffered the same fate.

It is necessary to restore these traditions and restore them to their original glory, as a sacred knowledge among the indigenous people who know how to keep it sacred. In ancient Mexico, there were many cultures which knew magic and mystery.

In Huautla there is still much of that tradition that is still safe from alien hands. The Mazatec healers have passed from generation to generation a knowledge that in ancient times transported the shamans to the world of magic of the gods.

13. DON RICARDO, THE HEALER FROM SANTA CRUZ

A friend named Guillermo took me to visit Don Ricardo, a healer from the nearby town of Santa Cruz. We arrived in the afternoon. My friend explained my interest in the magic mushrooms and Don Ricardo accepted to make a ceremony. We began to make the necessary preparations while the sun was going down.

We started the ceremony. Don Ricardo began to sing after we had completed all the preliminaries. His song mixed the Mazateca language and Spanish with Christian themes. One of the litanies went as follows:

Oh Maria Madre mia
Oh consuelo del mortal
Amparadme y llevadme
A la Patria Celestial

Oh Mary, Blessed Mother
Consolation of the mortal being
Give me protection and transport me
To the Celestial Plane.

Don Ricardo sang with deep feeling and sweetness. I reacted to this verse with a very strong emotion. After a few hours, he turned to me and said:

-You made a trip outside the country. You went to the United States and Canada, right?

This was not the first time someone surprised me with a revelation that I had not mentioned to them.

-Yes.

Guillermo asked him how he knew.

-I just saw it in my trip. I saw you sitting in the plane with others passengers. I could smell the fabric of the seats and I knew that you were going to the United States. I saw it in the flame of the candle...

He had a candle lit in front of him and he looked at it fixedly. Guillermo and I were at a loss.

-I see your parents have passed away. You should say a mass for their eternal rest. Heed me and have the mass said. It will help them greatly.

I had never told Guillermo anything about my parents. There was not any way that Don Ricardo could have known from him that my parents had died.

I noticed that his technique involved concentration on the candle to use his powers. But he introduced me to a new technique that I had not seen anybody use before: dance. After his last remarks, he broke into a dance that he performed while he sang. He moved rhythmically at the same time that he sang.

He was a picture of harmony, sound and movement. The litanies were slow and full of sweetness, the dance was rhythmic and slow. It created a sense of satisfaction in us to watch. He later said to Guillermo:

-That girl is not meant for you. She has another lover and she is unfaithful to you. You will better off forgetting her,

Guillermo had told me about his girl friend and that he had doubts about her. We were both very intrigued by Don Ricardo's revelations about us. It was a lesson in the powers of the mushrooms from a man who had not formal education, no material wealth nor other signs of success.

14. THE DREAM TO AN ENCHANTED PLACE

I returned to Mexico City and took his advice. I asked for a mass in memory of my parents.

One night in the city, I had a dream that took me to the sierra. I was home and I began to dream that I was watching the horizon. There was a beautiful landscape in the distance. A lonely place which was far away particularly attracted my attention. I could barely make it out as a speck on the face of the far away mountains.

I had a feeling that this place would unlock some secrets for me. Using my will, I transported myself directly to that far away place.

I sat down in the valley, next to the rocks. I was totally alone, and my state of mind was calm, peaceful. I was in ecstasy and expecting something wonderful.

I did not know exactly what I was waiting for. But I was waiting something that would give me light, peace and power. In the meantime I was observing the place where I was.

It was clearly visible how the erosion had worn out the soil. It was dry and the rocks were all around me. The trees were in the distance and the sun was brightly lighting the whole valley.

I felt as if I had eaten the mushrooms. But the next moment I felt that I WAS THERE. It was not just a dream. All my sensations were direct touch with my environment out in the mountains.

I kept telling myself: "This is not a dream."

Other times when dreaming I knew that it was so. This time was different because I was totally awake in this state. I do not know how long I remained there but the sun went down and I remained there through the night. The full moon came out in all its glory and the stars came next. The following day I saw the sun rise and reach its zenith. I continued sitting there as if there was nothing else to do.

All physical sensations of tiredness, hunger, thirst were absent. I was in a place where peace and tranquility were total, there was not disturbance, and I was free to inspect my life and contemplate my place in the cosmos.

I then felt desire to return to Mexico City and with an act of will I returned to my bed where I awoke with the conviction that I had been away in the valley and had returned to the city.

I am now convinced that the trip was an astral voyage when my soul simply left its body and I was free to travel at will without physical limitations.

Months later I returned to the Hill of Worship. I made my offer of seven grains of cacao, and I sat down to contemplate the landscape. I saw the valley from there. It was my first time looking that place. But I could recognize the valley and I felt the same attraction to that place as in my dream.

María Sabina, photo by Juan Peralta

15. DEATH OF MARIA SABINA

In November 1985 I returned to the Sierra. On the 23rd I was walking with a group of tourist from the landing strip to the iron bridge. One of them told us:

-Did you know that Maria Sabina died last night?

I had often heard rumors of her dead in the past, but they had always proved false. This time I knew that she was very old and had been sick. Although the news was unexpected, I knew they were true when I heard. It took me altogether by surprise, however, and my tears began run.

-Are you sure?

-She died last night in the Social Security Hospital in Oaxaca. The news came out in the newspapers. She is going to be buried in Huautla tomorrow.

Next day I went to the town square. In the City Hall, there was a coffin with the remains of the Great Priestess. The town people had shown up to pay their respects. All the people had been surprised and they were worried.

Her picture was placed over the coffin. All the press reporters, the common people, men, women and children were present to pay homage to the old lady who had placed the town of Huautla on the map and who had given all great examples of love and humility. They came to show their love and respect.

There was infinity of flowers surrounding the simple coffin. The police made an honor guard around the coffin and the mourners did the same in the outer perimeter.

I joined the crowd. The whole town was moved by the grief of losing their finest citizen. She had given so much to her home town and to her country. It is true that prophets are not appreciated in their homeland; she had been recognized by foreign scientist before her own countrymen, except on this day.

Several speakers took the floor to recall her accomplishments, drawing attention to the specific powers that had been her sign of mastership. Some drew attention to her international fame and how she had astounded unbelievers.

The ceremony was simple, afterwards we all gathered to escort the coffin to the cemetery. The funeral cortege was led by a band since the Mazatecs always bury their dead with music. At the cemetery there were other speakers. I decided to speak also, since many of the earlier speakers had only drawn attention to the petty personal jealousies that attend people of accomplishment.

-I want to say how young people like me feel about having had the privilege of meeting with Maria Sabina. We were with her in her ceremony, and we came here to Huautla just to meet her, her fame brought us here, young people in search of God. And we found in Maria Sabina one of the great adepts in her ceremony of the sacred mushrooms. She is one of the last adepts of pre-Hispanic knowledge. She is the example that Mexico has not changed and that great treasures can still be found here even after four centuries of Spanish influence. The Indians still nurture their culture, their beliefs, the wisdom of their gods; the Mazatecs are an example of this.

-Maria Sabina astounded foreign and Mexican born alike. Huautla should be proud that one of its own achieved such a status because she is a symbol of our own culture and of things that are purely Mexican. Her shining spirit led us to find ourselves, to find God within, in these mountains full of wonder.

-There is no doubt that God wanted to take her to His Garden to regale her with flowers and colorful singing birds so that she can add her special talent, her song to the Garden of Eden.

-Maria: you are with God but all those who knew you through your ceremony will always remember you with affection and gratefulness. You were a great woman, a priestess. We are proud of you, especially because you bring to us timeless wisdom from our Indian forebears, their wisdom that has been forgotten or underestimated by the ignorant. All who ridiculed you were not content, they also stopped to misrepresenting your accomplishment and to exploit your talent, but now they will have to hide their faces in shame because you have now passed on to the judgment of History.

-Thank you Maria for your ceremony, your song, your humility, your smile and your wisdom. Thanks you for receiving the young who were anxious to know you even in your humble house. We will never forget you. May God be with you and bless you…

One of the grandchildren gave me a handkerchief to wipe away my tears which by now were overflowing. Someone turned a cassette player on and we heard for the last time that day her shamanic song.

Maria Sabina
Mural painting by the author

16. REMEMBERING OF MARIA SABINA

She was the most celebrated shaman of the Mazatec tradition. She is the most prominent personality in the field of traditional medicine.

Born in 1888, she lived a life of poverty no different from her neighbors. Nevertheless, she was the heir of the timeless wisdom of her forebears, whose practices predated by centuries the Spanish conquest. This wisdom comprised the ceremonial use of the magic mushrooms, for the purpose of healing the sick.

The tradition is pure Mazateca, and its origins are lost in antiquity. The reason the tradition has survived is because of the miraculous results attained by the shamans. The tradition has been passed orally down to our present days.

Maria Sabina was recognized internationally after Gordon Wasson wrote about his experiences in Oaxaca. He visited the Mazateca region in the fifties and spent several years studying the mushrooms ceremony of Maria Sabina and published several books and monograms on the subject.

After being introduced to the world, so to speak, she became internationally famous for her knowledge and experience with the healing powers of the mushrooms. Many beat a path to her humble house, both locals and foreigners alike, all in search of a cure for their physical or spiritual ailments.

She was wise counselor and a seer. According to her, she did not heal. God worked the miracles though the ceremonial use of the sacred mushrooms. This is the secret of the tradition. She acquired the requisite knowledge and developed it to a degree of mastership. She became recognized as the High Priestess of the mushrooms ceremony.

Other members of the scientific community besides Wasson also bore witness to her genuine healing powers, such as Albert Hoffman and Roger Heim. Famous anthropologists also wrote about her, such as Fernando Benitez and Gutierre Tibon.

Visitors to Huautla who came to see her in the sixties included Walt Disney and the Beatles.

Years after the Beatles broke up, John Lennon and Yoko Ono went to see her in the seventies. After one of his visions, John told Yoko that he had just seen his death by assassination. Years later, the vision was borne out.

One of the wonders that the sacred mushrooms confer is the power to see the past and the future. The shamans use these powers to identify the causes of illness and to find the cures.

When I went to see Maria Sabina in 1972, I stayed at her home several weeks and became acquainted with her family, daughters and grandchildren. They were very poor and they work hard. She used to gather firewood, harvest coffee, tended the fields, straightened out and cleaned her own house, tended sick visitors, looked after her grandchildren, gave advice, took decisions and ordered her life with true mastership.

In the afternoons, Maria Sabina showered. One of the daughters would place a chair outside facing towards the mountains. Her hair was combed for hours while she contemplated the mountains in the distance. She was lost in silence and meditation and the combing of the hair was a full ritual which never varied. Her wrinkled face was evidence of the harshness of life in the mountains but it also was evidence of her age and made her look wise.

She had a good vista of the mountains from the place where she lived, "El Fortín", about two hours above Huautla close to the Hill of Worship. Her house was on the way to the altar on the Hill.

As the sun began to set and the stars to show themselves in the darkening sky, Maria Sabina was fully combed with her familiar tress, tinged with grey and white. She would stand up, thanked her daughter, and with a generous smile would ask me to go inside and have a cup of coffee.

Her house was lit with yellow candles of pure virgin wax. Her adobe house did not have electricity; it had a roof covered with thin corrugated metal sheets. One permanent feature of her life was the constant chatter of her daughters and grandchildren in their native language. She spoke little, but when she talked, everyone would keep silent and listen with respect.

The international visitors did not seem to face her and she carried herself as if the news abroad of her accomplishments were far away and inconsequential to her daily life.

On occasions, I would buy cigarettes, brad, honey, milk, eggs and other groceries. I handed her the bag with the groceries and she only took the cigarettes and a piece of brad and handed the rest to her grandchildren. Her grandchildren reminded me of a brood of chicks revolving around the mother hen. When night arrived, the little old lady who had patiently borne the daily chores and dealt with people much younger than herself turned into a priestess of the ancient tradition, the woman seer and healer.

She wore a dark blue *rebozo* for the ceremony and she lit candles. She became solemn and quiet; she looked like a saint. The light of the candles transfigured her. She placed the sacred mushrooms in earthen plates for the participants and began to pray in Mazatec. The names of Jesus Christ, Saint Peter and Saint Paul were interspersed throughout her prayers. When the mushrooms were consumed, the physical world was left behind and the participants entered the world of the spirit. In her own words: "I take the person who communes with the sacred mushrooms to where God is." Her shamanic chants were intense and emotional to the extreme and evoked strong spirituality.

Maria Sabina lifted the veil of mystery surrounding the Mazatec tradition. Her effectiveness proved her to be genuine and made it possible to take seriously an unwritten tradition which is still not fully understood. It made it clear to all who would see that the shamans of Oaxaca are heirs to a timeless wisdom with strong healing power based on traditional medicine. The medium is sacred or medicinal plants. The passing of Maria Sabina does not end the tradition because there are others who have learned it and carry it on and who treasure it as the most precious bequest from their forebears.

I lived with Maria Sabina and deal with her daily, we ate together, conversed and I learned from her. Her knowledge was deep and full of mystery. One day, I sat on the floor of her house and tried to stand a candle up, and the candle fell. I noticed her gaze and she laughed and looked away. She then took the candle from my hands and effortlessly placed it standing on the floor. I realized that she had been tipping the candle over when I tried to stand it up.

It was powers like this she brought out during her ceremony in order to discover the past and the future, and the illnesses of the sick. I do not know how it did; I can only declare what I saw. She also had the ability to change her expression and she could look like a mean witch or like a chaste saint. She had many facets to her personality, she had personal authority and power, and she was mysterious. I learned to admire her and to love her for the great good she did to me: it was through her and the ceremony that I learned about God and came to know Him.

She was easy to love. She was generous with all and full of grace; she was a noble teacher and humble. The first impression she gave was of sanctity and love, for despite her solemn ritual, in the day she was happy and she had glint in her eye. Her life had been harsh and difficult but she was a true master.

To me she was a teacher, a priestess, a counselor and a friend. She was my inspiration to talk and write about the sacred mushrooms. My research into the Mazatec tradition made me appreciate the ancient cultures which lived in Mexico before the conquest. I came to see her as the symbol of the timeless Mexico which offers still a deep mystery going beyond pure intellectual research. I saw her also as the humble representative of all the faceless individuals who take up the calling to carry on the tradition in the Mazatec Sierra.

17. SPIRITUAL SOLITUDE AND MYSTICISM

All the experiences led me away from people and led me to the solitary path in search of God. When I went to Huautla for the first time I styled myself a Marxist, an atheist, a skeptic and intellectual.
My direct encounter with the world of the magic of the sacred mushrooms Teonanacatl made me feels the Spirit Within, and then God. Thanks to the state of mind produced by Teonanacatl I recognized the great lie in which we live when we separate ourselves from nature and from god.

Human society is blind and lost in a maze of egoism and material ambition, people simply forget their self and forget god, just to pursue material success.
We are on the brink of atomic destruction. Man has lost his way and has sunk deeper and deeper into a morass of materialism, forgetting all sign of spiritual and moral values.

This realization led me to find refuge in spiritual aloofness, trying to get away from the mundane garbage of egoism and ambition. Nations make war in response to dark motives found in ambition and evil. Men eat each other like wild beasts in their frenzy for material gain. Man takes his measure by his material success, by checkbook, without taking measure of his knowledge or his creativity. Many great men have been ignored by their contemporaries to live in poverty and obscurity.
War is a crime against Man and man's worst crime against Divine Justice. War is de denial of all that is good and beautiful in man, gifted by God.

The day men denied the God of Love, of Light and of Peace, who sustains the Universe, they denied their Greater Self, and they plunged into a fog. Nevertheless, there have been men of such ignorance and blindness that they made war in the name of religion. What absurd logic.

They worshipped bloody and cruel gods in lieu of worshipping the One True God of Love. Within the spirit of each man there glows the spark of Divine Light, which when allowed will radiate love and understanding. It is our mystical essence.

In order to find our mystical essence, it becomes necessary to live alone and to leave the crowd, to leave civilization behind, and to find the truth within Nature. Civilized life leads us away from God.

Through the sacred mushrooms I understood that God exists, that the spirit within man is immortal and forever. I do not try to say that this is the only path to God, it is only one, and I followed it. I lived in the mountains.

All the paths which we follow with love serve to raise our consciousness. The surrender to love means that we do our work without causing harm to our neighbor and that we surrender to our path with sincerity and conviction.

It is my lot to live in a time when all that I believe in is rejected. Nevertheless in the aloofness of the spirit it is possible to find God. In the midst of civilization, with its noise and its temptation, it is easy to find evil. That is why I love the mountains, the rivers and the lonely valleys, the oceans, all that reminds one of the lost Eden and which humanity has worked to destroy.

Man finds his best within the peace of Nature. Man was created to live among the trees, the wild birds, warmed by the sun, inspired by the stars, voyaging through mountains and forests. This understanding led me away from men and led me to live a solitary life. It is very few who truly accept that the spirit is eternal, that it will survive our physical death, and that our true essence is spiritual and eternal, in other words, to live forever.

We are cosmic voyagers, spirits that have been here in one form or another since the day that creation began. We have been stones, plants, trees, fish, reptiles, different animals, and men, in other eras of creation. This is not the first time we are here, but it will be neither be the last.

Only in solitude of my own spirit have I been able to find the Light of God. Many will misunderstand because I found this understanding through the sacred mushrooms, but at the same time they do not know the mushrooms or its proper use. They would become surprised when the mushrooms are mentioned, but they are not troubled when considering alcohol or wars a normal experience.

They will not condone those who use the mushrooms, but they will not bother to find out the truth about it, thinking it is merely a drug.

That is why I went away, without trying to convince anyone. The world is too much affected by war and materialism to spend a little time on God.

We have to find ourselves within nature. This is the answer that I found. Mysticism is to search for the Light and Love of God.

18. WORSHIPPING THE ETERNAL FATHER

Teonanacatl made me understand that we share in a divine essence, that we are eternal and infinite. Teonanacatl changed my life when I was able to view the world of sacred things. It is so infinite this world that books could be written about it, which could never hope to exhaust its description.
Worship of the Father in human history has found many diverse forms; religious symbols and rituals have been invented around this ideal. Teonanacatl is one of them.

The Mazatecs have build up an entire religion around the sacred mushrooms. While all religions are different, they are all forms of worshipping the One True God, you can find a common symbolize pointing to the Sun as the only fit symbol of the Great Divinity.

From the Sun issues the divine energy. The Sun cult is the synthesis of all the religions. All the people have recognized the Sun as the symbol of God, of his energy that maintains us and of his light that raises our consciousness.

The rays of the Sun are cosmic energy; they flow lovingly to Mother Earth and make her fruitful, making life in the planet possible.

The shamanic ceremonies of the Mazatecs are held facing the East, facing the point from which the Sun will rise. The sacred mushrooms owe its life to the combination of Sun and Earth, assisted by the god of rain, *Tlaloc*. The mushrooms are therefore the synthesis between cosmic energy and telluric energy.

Our ancestors the Aztecs worshipped *Tonatiuh*, the Sun god, of the essentials gods. Thanks to him they knew that Creation had been made possible, his light and his energy were a representation of the Divine Love. It is to the direction of Sun, the East that we have to direct our prayers, thanking him for all that is freely given to us.

We must pray for forgiveness to Nature for all our sins, separately we must beg forgiveness from the Sun, the Moon, the Earth, the sea, the Mountains, the Rivers, the Trees, the Clouds. We have to beg forgiveness from the bottom of our hearts for all the harm that we have caused to our neighbor and to all living things.

Every time we have an opportunity to view the Sun at its rising, we ought to bless him and thanks him for his Divine Rays. And when we view him at sunset, we must promise to continue our work to become perfect, to become more worthy of his love.

The solar cult is the fundamental essence of the white magic, of all true knowledge. In Man's heart there glows a spark of solar energy. That is the reason why we can love. Love is solar energy, lighting and making fertile all it radiates on.

The Sun is our father, the Earth is our Mother, and the Moon is our wet nurse. We are children of god and our mission is to assist Our Father on Earth to continue His Creation. We must become instruments of our father's will, helping to make his love and his light known. We must learn to love all living things, and to return our planet to that blessed era when it was a true Garden of Eden, where blessed birds will sing as before and where peace and harmony will reign. All men must learn to live as brothers, since that is what we are: spiritual brothers, without prejudice towards races or religions, united only in one common goal: universal love and harmony flowing throughout the Universe.

This will be the awakening of Humanity, the bird of a cosmic brotherhood.

19. HEALING PRAYERS

To Jesus Christ

Oh highest master of Humanity
Hope to all on Earth
Your exemplary life and your teachings
Hold the best hope for Man.

You are the light of God,
You, who came to the world to give light.
Humanity needs you more today
In this time of fog, war, hate and tears.

The Earth is lost without you.
Man stumbles blind and insane
Without your light, your word,
And your example.

Perhaps we are not deserving, but if you will,
Return to Earth.
Show yourself if only an instant.
A sign will suffice, an instant of your divine presence
To awaken man from darkness.

I beseech you in the name of the hungry children,
Of the sick mothers, of the old who are sad
And alone, of the sick in the soul, of the sick in the body,
Of the blind and those mutilated in war.

We all need your word, your presence,
Your hands which console and heal.

Send us the Light of the Father
To help us recover hope.
Make us feel your divine presence
To begin to believe in man and in Earth anew.

Protect us, help us, save us.
Being close to you is living in the light and eternally
With your smile and your peace
Which were with you even in the cross.
Holy you are always.

Hopefully someday Humanity
Will be worthy of a guide and a master like you.

Amen.

Prayer for the Human Good.

Jesus, kind and generous
Transcending all men and all races
For all time.
Our big brother.
Holy, blessed by all men.

Help us to live in the world of love and fraternity,
A real sky, not just a cold and indifferent blue
When contemplating human suffering.

Thank you for teaching us to cultivate the land
And to make the dough for bread with love
And to warm our body and our heart
With compassion and gentleness.

You always say how we must repay with love
Those whom we have made to suffer
So that in loving we become worthy of your forgiveness
And our peace within.

You know that with understanding,
We will be able to strive against negative passions,
Hardness of heard and cruelty,
Since your love not only liberated us from evil
But also made us more like you.

We will strive tirelessly to become worthy of you

So that always be so.

Amen.
Litany on the Blood of Christ.

Lord God, have pity on us.
Jesus Christ, have pity on us.
Lord God, have pity on us.

Jesus Christ, hear us
Jesus Christ helps us.
Lord God of Heaven,
Have pity on us.
Son God Redeemer of the world
Have pity on us.

Son God Redeemer
Of the world
Have pity on us.

God Holy Spirit
Have pity on us.
Holiest Trinity, You are one God
Have pity on us.

Blood of Christ,
Son of the Eternal Father
Save us.

Blood of Christ,
Logos of God made flesh
Save us.
Blood of Christ, of the New Testament,
Save us.

Blood of Christ, flowing in agony
over the Earth,
Save us.

Blood of Christ, on seeing you at the flagellation,

Save us.

Blood of Christ, which flowed from the crown of thorns
Save us.
Blood of Christ, price of our salvation,
Save us.

Blood of Christ, spilled on the Cross,
Save us.
Blood of Christ, without which there is not redemption,
Save us.

Blood of Christ, purified and consumed in the Eucharist
Save us.
Blood of Christ, treasure of mercy
Save us.

Blood of Christ, triumphant over death and over evil,
Save us.
Blood of Christ, fortress of the martyrs,
Save us.

Blood of Christ, strength of the confessors,
Save us.
Blood of Christ, source of virginity,
Save us.

Blood of Christ, hope of those in danger,
Save us.
Blood of Christ, salve of the suffering,
Save us.

Blood of Christ, consolation of our tears,
Save us.
Blood of Christ, consolation of the dying,
Save us.

Blood of Christ, source of eternal life,
Save us.
Blood of Christ, peace for all hearts,

Save us.

Blood of Christ, who save the souls from Purgatory,
Save us.

Lamb of God, who takes away the sins of the world,
Forgive us, oh Lord
Lamb of God, who takes away the sins of the world,
Have mercy of us.

Amen.

Prayer of the precious Blood of Christ Jesus

Oh Lord God who redeemed all men
By the precious blood of Your Son.
Sustain in us the wonderful work of your forgiveness
So that, in celebrating constantly
The mystery of our salvation,
We may be able to attain its fruit,
Offering with all humility our own life in exchange
As Your will is done in ourselves.
Cleanse us always with the blood of our Savior
So he may become for us
The fountain of Eternal Life.

Amen

Prayer to the Solar Logos

Thou, Solar Logos, emanation of fire,
Christ in essence and consciousness.,
Potent life with which all progresses,
Come unto me and penetrate me, give me light, bathe me,
impale me and awaken in me the I Am
all these ineffable substances,
so much a part of thee, as of myself.

Universal and Cosmic Force
Mysterious energy,
I call on thee! Come unto me!
And remedy my affliction.

Heal me of this evil and part me from this suffering
so that I can attain harmony, peace and health,
I beseech Thee on Thy Holy Name,
Which Mysteries and the Gnostic Church have taught me,
to make vibrate in me
All the Mysteries on this
And higher planes, and that, combined, all these forces
May achieve the miracle of my healing.

Amen

All kind of prayers are utilized by the healers with wonderful effect on the ill. They all must be said with deep sincerity and faith. With the prayers one can cure anyone, including one self. They must be recited looking towards the East, and burning incense or copal. They must be repeated as many times as necessary to attain the cure.

20. SONGS OF MARIA SABINA

I am a woman who cries
I am a woman who speaks
I am a woman who gives life
I am a woman who strikes
I am a spirit woman
I am a woman who shouts
I am a woman of the air
I am a woman of light
I am a pure woman
I am a doll woman
I am a bird woman
I am the Jesus woman

I am the heart of Christ
I am the heart of the Virgin
I am the spirit woman
I am the doctor woman
I am the moon woman
I am the interpreter woman
I am the star woman
I am the heaven woman

I am Jesus Christ
I am Saint Peter
I am a saint
I am a saint woman
I am the heart of the Father
I am the woman who waits
I am the woman who struggles
I am the woman of victory
I am the woman of thought
I am the Creator woman

NAHUATL POEM

Here is what you must work and do
Held abeyance, shut away
It was left by our elders when they left them
With the white hair and the wrinkled face
Our precursors
They came not to be arrogant
They came not looking with anxiety
They came not to be rapacious
There were such
That they have honor
They reached the grade of tigers and eagles.

OUR LADY OF HUAUTLA

Maria, mother of the new God, Jesus Christ
Sabina, the wise one, old goddess *Yololcitl*, the healer of the night
Your ceremony is the rite, the communion of men with their gods,
Man with his God.
Maria, softly, solemnly, is the wise one and the healer
Holy One.
Dead and risen through the Flesh of Our Lord Jesus Christ
Teonanacatl
Healer, she who knows the thousands of vegetable miracles,
e herbalist of the millennium.

In the ceremony you lose consciousness of the insignificant human form,
And you can reach unanticipated spiritual pinnacles.
Mystical ascension, ecstasy, cosmic madness, lights, flowers, colors, the Garden of Eden.

Indian priestess who impelled me to God with your gentle song,
Holy and blessed you are,
Where ever you are.

Amen

PART 2:
THE MAGIC OF MAZATEC SHAMANS

21. THE SHAMAN OR EAGLE WARRIOR

Traditional medicine and shamanism are part of a universe of knowledge which requires years of study and application, due to the depth of the subject.

I seek to go further into the subject of magic and wisdom of the Mazatecs, not from the viewpoint of scientific research, but from the subjective personal approach of a student who is free from the restrictions that academic disciplines often enforce on the mind.

Beyond the adventure of sensual experiences is the true knowledge, wisdom, which is available to anyone who partakes of the magic mushrooms. For the initiated, the magic mushrooms is an entity affectionately known to the shamans as the Holy Children, it is the equivalent to the host in religious meaning in that it is a spiritual medicine to heal the body, the mind and the soul.

The wisdom of the Mazatec shamans is a limitless source of nourishment from which I have partaken during the past twenty years, and I continue to marvel at the magic and wonders which emanate from it. Each day I continue to marvel at the mysteries which are revealed to me by the sacred ground in Huautla.

I have truly adopted these beautiful mountains and this Indian culture to such a degree that more than half my life has been spent traveling and living here. The journey has been worth the effort.

Before I continue, it is helpful if I explain what a "shaman" is. The world itself comes from the Siberian region, meaning medicine men. But it has now been applied to many practitioners throughout the world.

One of the names by which the shamans are known is the *"eagle warrior"*, and in Mazatec language, *"shota shine"*, that means the wise ones, seers, or healers. The shaman is a priest, a healer, an exorcist and a seer. The four powers are his tools and his knowledge.

One of the healers I knew told me that the healers are warriors because they face evil spirits sometimes during the mushrooms ceremonies and must fight them for the soul of the sick and that the eagle refers to the spiritual heights that must be reached before they can heal others.

The four forms of knowledge of the eagle warrior are:

The priest is the one who performs the ritual, sanctifies all the transcendental acts in the lives of individuals, the families and the community. He sanctifies the planting, the harvest, the weddings, the births and the burials.

The healer knows the secrets of diagnosis and applying medicinal plants to the suffering of his neighbor.

The exorcist, expels the evil spirits and fight sorcery. He can face evil spirits that take the souls of people hostage and defeat them with prayer and chant.

The seer delves into the past and the future of people, can determine their degree of spiritual evolution, and can see and treat the spirits who live in the astral plane.

The four forms of knowledge and power may be exercised at any time for one person or for the good of all. The eagle warrior is a teacher and a wise counselor. But before he or she can be effective, the warrior must be one who lives in sanctity, observing of the laws of abstinence. The warrior must live cleanly before God, free from evil and from contamination of the body or soul. Such dedication leads to the development of the power to see and the individual acquires power in the spiritual world to command. Evil spirits do not obey unless the one commanding is totally pure and holy. During the ceremony the healer can see the disturbances and command them with his words to heal.

The chants are an integral part of the ceremony which every shaman does according to his own style. The chants also confer the power to see and to heal. The chants further strengthen the power of the shaman to see, heal and command, and to invoke the Spirit and power of God. The shamans do not take credit for the result, they all affirm that the Spirit of God is the power that heals the sick and they are only the vessel through which God works.

The Mazatec shamans use these forms of knowledge. I have seen miraculous cures and other wonders.
I have participated in research of a purely personal nature, at first as a witness and observer, later as a participant and beneficiary, and finally as an apprentice.

I remain eternally grateful to God for allowing me to have access to the wisdom of the Mazatecs. My experiences have been real, not just vicarious nor theoretical. My writing is therefore a testimony to the things that I have witnessed which transcend rational explanations and leads to the connection of human consciousness directly to the Consciousness of God.

The shaman operates in this rarefied where ceremonies and healing take place, before they can manifest in the physical plane.
Not unwillingly, destiny has converted me into a messenger of this sacred knowledge, which is in danger of extinction. It is a dignified task which requires a total commitment. It is very similar to the work of a miner who searches avidly in his pan for the golden flecks.

I am a searcher for hidden treasures, wisdom lost or hidden in the shamanic tradition of the Mazatecs. I feel duty bound to share this treasure with all my brothers, especially with you, the reader, with the highest love from above.

22. THE MAGIC HUMMINBIRD

In the summer of 1993, I went back in the Mazatec Sierra with the intention of continuing my research.
In the woods and the mystery, at the pinnacle of the Hill of Worship, I was that day. I was sitting on the ground, contemplating the vastness of the surrounding mountains and awed by their vastness.

I saw materialize in front of me a magical being, beautiful like a hummingbird, who began to sing with great intensity, all the time his gaze fixed on me while remained suspended in the air in front of me. He was singing for me. After an instant, he left me.

I was speechless and surprised, deep in thought.

He reappeared singing once again, suspended in the air. This time he went flying among the trees. It was clear to me that he was trying to convey a message for me.

The third time he returned, he fixed his gaze on me while singing right in front of me, and left for good.

After he left, silence invaded my mind. It dawned on me that the Spirit of the Mountain was welcoming me like an old friend that you have not seen in a while. I sensed a gentle reproach for not coming sooner. He said:

-I know you since a long time ago. Your spirit already belongs to the magic and the power of the mountains. You must remain in the mountains so you can learn to fly like an eagle.

My eyes moistened with tears. I took a fistful of dirt in my hand and squeezed it. The wind began to blow around me and I understood that the Spirit was with me.

I looked up and saw three eagles flying majestically above the altar of the Hill of Worship. A powerful voice from within made me understand the transcendence of the message. At that moment I decided to take control of my life and to become an apprentice to a shaman, an eagle warrior.

I vowed to myself: I must return to this magic place, to continue the search for sacred knowledge. That is the destiny laid out by my heart. Besides, I cannot forget my vow to find God in an enchanted place, among the mountains.

I thanked Our Father, with my heart moved to gratefulness for the opportunity to return to the sacred land where He had spoken to me for the first time.
I resolved to follow the voice within and my mystical vocation in the mountains with the intention of finding God, to be with Him day and night, to sense His Spirit within my beating heart.

Photo by Luis Miguel Ávila

23. THE WONDERS OF THE MAZATEC SIERRA

The day lays its veil of white clouds, wrapping the Sierra like a bride on her wedding day.
The mountains are overlaid with cotton while the dying sun lights up the sky with blotches of pink and orange gently dabbing at the clouds.

The night descends on the mountains with the inscrutable mystery of the dark, and reveals the stars one by one in the majestic silence of the sky.
After the timeless of the contemplation of the night, the adobe house is a welcome resting place for the solitary hermit.

The blazing fire protects consoles and gives company. Fragrant coffee sweetened with virgin honey, a simple gift from mother Earth. The smoke from the cigarette rising in constant spirals providing a balm for old memories and shooting the mind from the interruption of stray thoughts.

The murmur of night's insects, cosmic vibrations, produce a loosening sensation sending me to the astral plane. The night becomes full of chasms and phantoms which fill the darks void, mystery falls on the unsuspecting like a heavy blanket.

Morning: a concert of songbirds, roosters, ravens and other birds singing their thanks to the Lord. The sun spreads his light over the tops of the mountains and burns the moist fog.
Men come out of their huts whistling as they go to work and say hello to all they meet.

Women light the heart fires and fetch water; the children paint the air with their laughter. The donkeys protest, the crows' crow and the dogs bark while the busy murmur of people couches the sharp noises.

Life begins every morning. The Mazatecs give God His due with their daily work.
The fields, the plantain trees and the coffee bushes give their fruit up to sustain the people who tend them. The bees make delicious honey.

The promised land of the Mazatecs gives all in generous amounts to her children and they turn offer gift of dance -*Nasho Losha*- "The Orange Blossom".
The women dance with sweetness displaying their long black hair, their brown skin glistening in the sun, large doe eyes, and beautiful multi color dress.

The gentleness of their language fills the air with music of its own which the wind carries from place to place.

This magic land is full of beauty and poetry; it is a fit home for the gods and their retinue, a bridge between Heaven and Earth, a cradle to the wise shaman healers who guard their inheritance from the eagle warriors with alacrity.

In this sacred land are juxtaposed two realities, everyday and magic, the one who supersedes rational understanding.

24. TWELVE CLANS OF EAGLE WARRIORS

In the dark of the night, twelve warrior clans met in a sacred place, out in the middle of the wooded mountains under the full moon. The ancient initiates of the Eagle Warriors came to the magic mountains; they searched for all eternity and found the bridge between Earth and sky, the home of the gods.

The Spirit of the Mountain in the shape of a hummingbird guided the *shota-shinee*, the shamans, through heavy woods and deep canyons, beneath the stars and the dark sky. Each clan had been searching for the mythical bridge for centuries, until the day they came together at the top of the sacred mountain from which all other mountains of the Sierra seem like playthings.

Twelve sacred fires were lit and their brightness brushed the surrounding trees. In the meantime, music made with drums and flutes filled the air, accompanied by a timeless rhythmic chant.

The *shota-shinee* presided over the collective ceremony blessing the *ndi-shi-jto*, the sacred mushrooms. The rising smoke from the copal sanctified the ground where they stood. An old *shota-shinee* wearing a ceremonial mask in the shape of an eagle began to dance while singing a beautiful chant.

His family began to dance with him: young warriors and beautiful maidens, children and older men and women. Soon, all the twelve clans joined in. The dance of the eagle generates a great power which envelopes all the participants.

Another *shota-shinee* placed a large crystal of copal in the fire, which provoked the fire to rise and emit a thick cloud of smoke with a sweet fragrance which evoked the Great Spirit of *Nina*, God.

The earth becomes energized with the vibration of the drums and the song rose to the sky. They invoked the Spirit of the Mountain, the spirit of the deer, and the hummingbird. When the moon reached its zenith, a deer with huge antlers appeared among them, and transformed himself into the fair haired god joining them in their dance. He spoke to them in gracious voice and talked about wisdom.

The spirits of Earth, Water, Air and Fire slowly joined them in turn until every being at the sacred mountain top was vibrating in rhythmic dance. The visible and the invisible melted into each other in rays of energy communed with Mother Earth and the stars.

This spectacle that only *Nina* God can contemplate in its splendor and He sent His angels with many blessings for all. That night and in that place **Twelve Clans** -*Nashinanda Natejao*- (now called Huautla) established their holy altar to worship God.

The chant and the dance lasted until the star Venus appeared in the sky, and when the sun rekindled his fire and lit up the mountains with the light of the day.

Sacred mushrooms from an Aztec Codex.

25. DOÑA JULIETA, THE EAGLE WARRIOR

Doña Julieta asked us to enter the adobe room which she uses for her ceremony. The room is dedicated to only this use and it is in the inside patio of the house.
There is an altar with Christian images, flowers, and a brazier for the copal, plates with the mushrooms of each participant, candles, cacao, San Pedro, and holy water. At the other end of the room, there are beds for each participant also.

Doña Julieta, everyone in town calls her "Ma Julia", sat on the floor by the altar. She lit up the candles and began to pray in her language and to bless the mushrooms.

-You cannot call them mushrooms, she said quietly but with authority. Their name is Holy Children. They are good to heal the body and to cleanse the soul.

She is a beautiful Mazatec woman, slight build and raven black hair, fine features, but with a penetrating look, like an eagle.

Ma Julia asks our names as she continues her prayer. This time I was accompanied by a group of Spanish tourists who had come solely to find out about the shamanic ceremony. It was two older ladies and two young men.

WE gave her our names and she repeated them as she passed the plates to each one. She told us to chew only with our front teeth, not with our molars, as we are not eating; the Holy Children are not food.

They have a strong taste, and they still have the odor of the earth. To chew slowly is part of the ritual and afterwards, to eat cacao beans. The taste of the cacao is stronger than the mushrooms and bitter, and in my case I had to make an effort to finish it.

Ma Julia waited in silence. She did not have any mushrooms for herself and I asked her why.

-I do not need them to accompany you, she said enigmatically.

After about twenty minutes, she put out the candle and the room became pitch black. Thousands of points of colored light began to appear, yellow, blue, violet, red and white.

Ma Julia continued her prayer, but she was not longer a pure Mazatec Indian but a *shota shine*, the wise woman of knowledge, a priestess to the goddess Yololcitl, the ancient healer of the night, the rightful owner of all enchantment, our Mother.

Everything of pre-Hispanic culture has by now infused my thinking and brings all associations to my mind in a different context; it reminds me of my own deceased mother, who spent so much of her life in the study of pre-Hispanic culture. Remembrance brings tears to my eyes.

One of the tourists takes me out of my revelry. She says that she can see a great tree full of leaves to her side; it is an ancient tree with large roots penetrating the ground to a great depth.

-You are that tree – says Ma Julia. You are healthy and you still have many years ahead of you…

Her intervention surprised me. Briefly I could glimpse the great tree beside the lady who had described it. It led me to the conclusion that humans are like trees: some are large, ancient and give shade; others are young, fragile and need care. The deep roots are spiritual roots anchored deep in the universe which permit our earthly presence to grow and give fruit. A tree without such anchoring cannot grow for long, nor give fruit, and soon dies.

The Spanish lady is obviously very religious and her tree is fruitful with deep roots.

One of the young men begins to talk. He says that he feels painful thorns on his feet since a long time ago.

-Each thorn is a suffering that you have felt – said Ma Julia. You have travelled a very rough road.

He admits it and he begins to cry. We could see his naked and vulnerable soul.

Ma Julia continued to blow softly over his feet and with her hand she began to pull out each thorn lovingly from his feet, until little by little he began to calm down.

We all felt the emotion as we watched his cure take place. That taught me that the soul is also vulnerable to the thorns and stones in the highway of life.

Ma Julia had been healing the soul of the young writer. The thorns were "real", even if we the participants could not see them. They, the patient and Ma Julia, could see them clearly and there was not rest until they were all removed. Lovingly she handled his feet and gently removed each thorn, throwing it far away from her and him.

I felt that healing must be a beautiful experience also for the healer since there are no bounds where their power ends. It is a high calling which calls for a superior spiritual achievement.

Ma Julia had this power; she was a real *shota shine,* a spiritual teacher, dedicated totally to her vocation. Her sweet and clear voice opened the way and shed the light on the consciousness of the patient.

Speaking with her later, she gave me a hint of her wisdom about what had transpired.

-During the ceremony, the Holy Children confer the power to heal. The healing is done with words. Everything that is said during the ceremony has power. When you are in the ceremony speak to God and He will listen. Tell Him all, all, and he will cleanse you. It is the sin within that makes you sick. Our sins bring us illness but if you confess to God, He will heal you, cleanse your body and your soul.

After these words, she then began to cleanse us with herbs. Each one stood up in turn and let her sweep the sweet smelling herbs over his body and face while we prayed together. In my turn, I felt the herbs gently touching my face with sweetness and love, my mind clearing and overall feeling a sensation of lightness. I felt clearly that the herbs took something with them and I felt much better and awake. When she finished, the herbs were thrown for the moment in a corner of the room.

Everyone agreed that they felt very good with the cleansing.

Ma Julia offered us bread, breaking a round loaf which she said was also part of the gift to God. It is a feast of the soul, a banquet of the spirit when you commune with the Holy Children. She also gave us coffee to drink, which her helper served us.

I was truly impressed with the personality and wisdom of Ma Julia. I saw her as an heir to the Eagle Warriors, to the night healer, a true *shota shine*. I asked her for permission to write about her someday and she graciously gave it.

The Spanish tourists were truly enchanted with all they had seen. They could not stop thanking Ma Julia referring to her with great respect. WE had all felt for a few hours the spiritual connection which exists between us all, and between us and the eternal Universe.

Thank you Ma Julia and may God bless you.

A SONG OF THE HEART

My father is the Sun, my Mother, the Earth.
My sacred name is Solar Tiger.
My childlike heart, a shaman's apprentice,
raises his voice in a morning song.

My body burst from earth like a wild flower,
in the midst of the wood and the mountain range.
My diamond soul, a kaleidoscopic crystal,
reflects the living colors of the Universe.

My heart is nourished by the nightly mysteries,
and gains his strength from the Sun and the love of the Earth.
An infinite expanding love from my breast flows,
and I laugh, cry, love, and sing a hymn to the dusk
invoking the enchantment of all that surrounds me.

I contemplate the miracle of the dawn
And welcome the Sun with a grateful dance.
Eternal moments vibrate within,
As I acknowledge the mystery of the Universe.

From my heart shoots out an eternal light of suns and galaxies,
This light is Love Within.
I will my chant to reach the Fountain of Light,
To call forth the Love of the Earth,
and to reflect the light of the furthermost stars.
My chant flows from the heart.

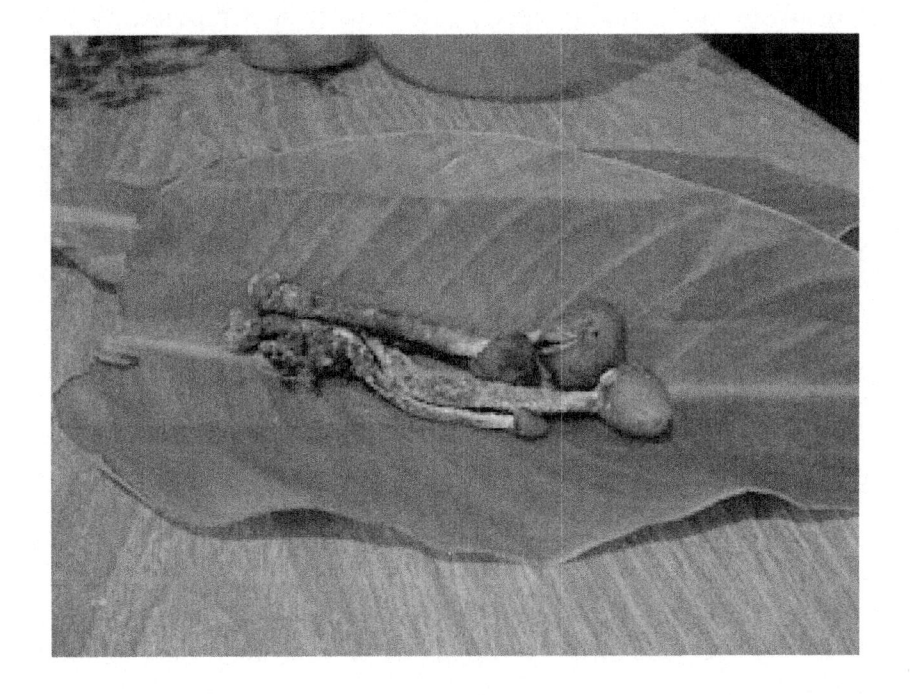

Photo by George Hartmann

26. THE HOLY CHILDREN

Ancient tradition requires fasting before taking the *Holy Children*. (Sacred mushrooms). One may however take fruit and water. It is also necessary to bathe and to wear clean clothing, preferably white or bright color, never black.

The *Holy Children* are taken at night, in a place consecrated with prayer, copal or incense, the candles of pure virgin wax, the powder of *San Pedro*, a book of prayers and faith. Faith is the fortress of the shaman. Faith is the weapon that sustains and strengthens in order to help face the tests and obstacles that emerge in the ritual.

If we have faith and prayer, and we are in a place that has been consecrated, the *Holy Children* can be taken without fear. They afford all the necessary protection from harm and provide all the wisdom of the Universe through Enchantment. Enchantment is magic, miracle and healing.

The most important aspect is the spiritual healing and cleansing that is conferred after the communion with the *Holy Children*. They also cleanse and heal the physical body, the mind and the soul of the participants, so that we can approach God.

It is necessary to observe five days of rigorous diet after the ceremony that is five days of holiness and respect towards God, without contamination in the form of sexual relations, eating pork, or drinking alcohol. It is also necessary to avoid inviting others to one's house to partake of meals or to visit another for the same purpose.

It is necessary to keep this regimen so that the healing process of the *Holy Children* takes place without interruption. In addition, the five day's observance after the ceremony is a personal sacrifice to become worthy of the miracles requested at the ceremony.

It is also important to speak to the *Holy Children* before taking them, as they are ready to listen. To address them with respect as one blesses them to permit us to enter the internal world through the communion. Within the physical reality of the mushrooms is an entity, a spirit of light, the spirit of the *Holy Children* who imparts the healing and the wisdom.

One needs to establish a dialogue with the *Holy Children:* if you ask them, they will respond.

They must be taken with love and respect, searching spiritual communion with God and His wisdom. When accomplished, this becomes the gift of the *Holy Children.*

As soon as the *Holy Children* are ingested, there is a celebration of the spirit. All sorts of spiritual beings attend the ceremony, relate to the Earth, the Air, Fire and Water. They come to celebrate and to have fun. Our gifts and sacrifices and prayers are in exchange for their good will. They are the Elementals, spirits, who nourish us and virtually keep us alive, since they are children of the Mother Earth. They come to play and it becomes necessary to receive them with joy, to welcome them, to be aware of their presence and to acknowledge them.

It is also necessary to make obeisance to the four cardinals' points: East, West, North and South. Each point has special energy which must be respected. The altar must face to the East, where the sun rises. The cult of the *Holy Children*, like Christianity, is a solar cult.

The way of the shamans who commune with the *Holy Children* is the way of solar magic. The Elementals have names in Mazatec, as follows:

Chicon Nangui..................Earth Spirits
Chicon Nanda...................Water Spirits
Chicon Tao......................Air Spirits
Chicon Lii.......................Fire Spirits

These are the sprits that come to the ceremony. The gifts that can be offered are cacao, flowers, candles, water. It is necessary not to be afraid of them. It is only needed to treat them with respect.

When the Elementals appear, they dance and play around the participants. They laugh and murmur to each other. The mushrooms are also children, spiritual beings of light; they are like little angels, like cherubim.

They are children of God. They command the Elementals and direct them to heal people. With the power of the Holy Spirit, the Children command everything under creation: other spirits in turn to listen and obey. Their action is miraculous and after they cause the healing to take place they also make it possible for us to feel God beating within.

The following prayers were revealed to me in a trance. They are a poem or litany dedicated to the Children, as if they were telling me what words are proper to use with them. In my case, the wonder is that the words were revealed to me in Mazatec, which I barely beginning to learn.

PRAYER OF *TI SANTOS*

Ti santos
Ti ndi shi to
Ti shote shine
Ti shota shine
Ti Nangi
Ti nanda
Ti Tao
Ti Lii
Ti Naitui
Ti Sa
Ti Nina
Ti Natjauna
Ti Nasho
Ti ndi shi to nasho
Ndi Santos
Nashecatshili
Ndali Nina
Ndali Padre Eterno
Nashecatshili

Ndali Jesus Christ
Ndali Lamb of God
Nashecatshili
Ndali Holy Spirit

Ndali White Dove
Nashecatshili

THE PRAYER OF THE HOLY CHILDREN

Holy Children
Children who grow
Healing Children
Children of the Earth
Children of the Wind
Children of the Fire
Children of the Sun
Children of the Moon
Children of God the Father
Children of God the Mother
Flower Children
Children who bloom like flowers
Holy Children
Thank you.

Good morning God
Good morning Eternal Father
Thank You

Good morning Jesus Christ
Good morning Lamb of God
Thank You

Good morning Holy Spirit
Good morning White Dove
Thank You

When I told Ma Julia about these words, she said that the spirit of the *Holy Children* was beginning to reveal wisdom to me, as they were beginning to talk in their secret language.

27. THE EARTH SPIRITS: *CHICON NANGUI*

Salvador, a Mazatec friend of mine, told me this story:

"The real owners of the land are not the people who live there. No it is not those who have the papers and pay the taxes. The real owners are the *blond ones*, the gnomes.

Chicon Nangui, that´s is their name. They are the Elementals of the earth. *Chicon* means blond, fair haired one, but it also means owner. *Nangui* means Earth.

When you build a house, you have to ask permission of the *Chicon Nangui*. You can´t pay with money, you have to use cacao, so they will let you build it. If you do not, there will be repercussions.

When I was a kid, I can barely remember, I used to see the *Chicons* in my house. I went outside for water, all of a sudden, there they were, right in front of me. My sister was thoroughly frightened one day. They used to pop out anywhere in the house. They are like little men, about three feet high but their features are pure Indian, Mazatecs. They are small, like midgets, and they walk around naked. Sometimes though, they dress up.

I saw them in the yard of my house. When you first see them, you get scared. But if you get over it, then you get curious. My mother used to see them when she was in the kitchen. She used to drop the earthen ware right then and there and run out to the kitchen screaming. Things went from bad and worse. They started appearing everywhere and at any hour of the day and night. We were all frightened; nobody dared go out at night, not even to piss.

My parents finally decided to call the priest and asked him to bless the house with holy water. That was the only way to get them under control. They stopped showing up and left us alone. We were finally able to get rest, no more frightful incidents. It's true I tell you I saw them!"

I heard many stories like this one. Doña Julieta told me about the time that they sent a boy for fire wood and he did not come back. They sent him early in the morning and he did not return for hours. They went to look for him, and could not find him until nighttime, crying out in the fields. He did not know why he ended up there not what exactly had happened to him. They had to perform a healing ceremony, and then he was OK:

-You see, when gnomes appear in a house, someone put them up to it. It is witchcraft.

They could also suddenly appear by themselves, but that only happens in unpopulated places, in places which are enchanted. As it just happened to me in the Worship Hill. Now that's a place that's full of magic and enchantment. I went there alone with the intention of communing with the sacred mushrooms. When I got to the altar, I placed my offer of cacao, flowers and one candle, and I also began to pray.

I took the *Holy Children* and went into the wood to find a solitary place near the altar. I sat down among the trees and waited. The Children began to work, and I suddenly became aware of the beauty of the mountains.

A thought, remembrance, came to me. I had dreamt about these woods before, even the pine trees which were on the other side of the mountain, and I got up and walked to that place. It was just as I had dreamt it!

I sat down and asked in a loud voice: "I wish to know why I have been here before in a dream"

I closed my eyes, expecting response. Nothing. Silence. I then see myself at the altar placing my offer there.

I slowly opened my eyes and saw right in front of me a little man, wearing a white shirt, looked like an Indian from the region. He was looking at me with great curiosity, but he was sitting sideways watching me out of the corner of his eye. In the flicker of an eye he melted into the tree itself and became the tree trunk, the branches and the leaves!
My God! I thought, I ran into a gnome. I looked around and saw at my left another little man, he was standing there with one amused look, and he was wearing nothing, and leaning against the tree trunk looking quite comfortable and relaxed with one leg crossed over the other. Suddenly, he too became the tree trunk, but this time he became the roots of the tree. I thought this was totally incredible!

As I raised my eyes, I saw three birds flying and coming to rest on the branch of a nearby tree. They began to sing. Off to the other side I heard several pine cones falling and rolling on the ground. It dawned on me that someone was having fun with me, like when you are distracted and someone flicks your ear and when you turn around, no one looks guilty.

The tree trunks made noise as is someone was shaking them, but I did not see anyone. I began to laugh when I realized that my question had been the catalyst for their games. I sat just watching and listening to the games of the gnomes as they continued to make friendly mischief in the woods.
I finally stood up and walked back to the altar, I thanked the Powers of the Mountain and left. I went back to town wondering if they were really children, mischievous and invisible. Or if they were really something else.

What I saw were like men, small in stature but men and they looked like Indians. I could not unravel that mystery.

They are not exactly nice. They will steal away a soul; they will make someone sick and kill, or make you insane. You need a spiritual force when you meet up with them, because an encounter is dangerous, and can be deadly.

Later on, my friends told me that they had been on their best behavior. They played with me and let me take a look of them. The gift at the altar had something to do with it.

DUSK

Rain, sky, the dying sun.
The wood, the silence of the clouds:
My soul crosses majestic landscapes,
Full of rain flowers and remembrances.

A rainy afternoon, melancholic and fresh,
My heart listens to the murmur
Of the wind among the trees.
Full of greenery, they play
With the raindrops on their leaves.

Thunder Mountain covered by clouds in the horizon.
Photo by Luis Miguel Ávila

28. THUNDER MOUNTAIN: *NINDO CHINKAO*

There is a mountain to the north of the state of Puebla called by the Aztecs *Ciciltepetl*. The Mazatecs called the Mountain of Thunder, *Nindo Chinkao*.

Only a very few of the shamans had the knowledge to approach to this mountain. Some of the peasants told me that there are many natural obstacles which make the climb next to impossible. The real obstacles are those that one cannot see.

The name of the mountain has a lot to do with the source of the thunderous storms, the fog and the cold in the Mazatec region. The people are afraid of it because it is associated with dark and terrible powers.

The Mazatecs are afraid and reverential towards this mountain at the same time. Some have attempted to scale it and have returned to say that they found it impossible, citing innumerable obstacles as well as disorientation. The locals believe that the difficulties cited by those adventurous enough to try are the result of approaching the mountain without the required reverence and or the needed offers to pacify the powers that be.

People do not realize the connection between spiritual cleanliness and the universe. They go to the Mountain without the required gifts and run into dangers that could be avoided with the right approach. There are stories of those who did not come back. The mountain is a place of great power. All the changes of the seasons are seen there first, and so are the storms of the region, the truly serious ones. It is the repository of the powers of the North. To the ancient cultures, the North represented *Mictlan*, the region of the dead. They also associated the North with all sorts of illnesses and evil powers.

I have also felt the curiosity to go to the Mountain and explore it myself. It is nearly always covered with fog and to me, mystery. It is the highest peak and the furthermost of the Mazatec region. Once when I was with a young Mazatec, I told him of my wish to explore the Mountain, and he told me:

-Don´t even try! It is the place of the Evil One! IT is his Mountain, where he lives. See, it is pure rock, no vegetation, it looks arid and deserted. You always see fog and it is cold. If *Nindo Chinkao* is the opposite of the *Hill of Worship*, it is the Mountain of Evil…

That only served to make me more curious. I found out that back in the 30's there was a crash of a Spanish plane. It was called *"The Four Winds"*. Only the army could go into the mountain to look for survivors, but they never found anything. Even thought the folklore says that the remains of the plane were found by locals and that they took the valuables without turning them over to the authorities, the crash only served to enhance the legend of the Mountain.

I had a different experience. In December 1994, I moved into town and located a house at the edge of the mountains directly facing *Nindo Chinkao*. The house was by the landing strip, where small airplanes and helicopters could land. This place has a commanding view of the mountains, particularly *Nindo Chinkao*.

On my first day I went out to look at the panorama. It was inspiring. That night I went to bed and tried to sleep. But when I closed my eyes, the Mountain dominated my view. I could see its details, the deep chasms, and I could feel the growling of the wind within its cavities. I felt a strong vertigo in my umbilical region, a horrible spiral force that pulled me towards the mountain. I felt that the force was not exerted on my physical body but on my astral body and that I was being pulled into a black hole that wanted to swallow me.

I covered my vulnerable region instinctively. I changed my position in bed and faced the South, pointing my head towards the East. The terrible sensation did not go away but it did diminish appreciably. I closed my eyes and felt how a strong wind gust lifted me up and took me to the Mountain. A light within told me that I was being dragged into another dimension. It was not a natural separation of my astral body from its physical form; it was the taking of a hostage, a form of spiritual kidnapping.

I stood up and lit a candle. I said a prayer asking for help and I began to feel a little calm. I went back to bed but did not go to sleep. I remained alert to the Mountain, which continued to pull me from time to time.

Next day I went to Doña Julieta and told her my experience. She said:

-The location of that house is very heavy. It faces directly north and there is no protection. You have dangerous currents emanating from that mountain. You must apply *San Pedro* dust in your umbilical region every night until those sensations disappear. The *San Pedro* closes up your body and protects you from assault. Never go out at night in that area when you have taken the Holy Children, better to put all that you need inside the house so you do not need to exit even to attend to your needs.

-What is going on, why can't I go out?

-Because you will attacked immediately by the Evil air. It carries illnesses.

I left Doña Julieta and thanked her for her assistance. I did as she told me to do and the sensation disappeared in a few days. I could sleep once again. The wind still roared outside, but I felt safe from the Mountain…

Altar in the Hill of Worship
(Photo by Luis Miguel Ávila)

29. THE HILL OF WORSHIP

The Hill of Worship is a sacred place. At its altar, I have experienced the Glory of God! It is such a wonderful place that there are no words to describe its light, its beauty, it harmony and peace. It is a natural altar.

Its name in Mazatec is *Chicon Nindo Tocosho*. At its peak, people come to pray to the Lord of the Mountain. The word *Chicon* means fair-haired one but it also means Owner or Lord.

It is a magic hill, full of strange power. It is inhabited by the elves or gnomes who have by their presence rendered it enchanted.

You must go to that hill with reverence and devotion. People who disregard that rule may have dangerous encounters since the hill is protected by spiritual guardians. They punish all who violate the rules or who come lightly or full of unrepentant sin.

The Lord of the Mountain is a fair-haired god who takes care of his people, who blesses them with health, strength and power. But he also brings illnesses and punishment to all those who are undeserving by their own actions, mainly failure to keep the rules of communion with the Holy Children.
Chicon is neither good nor bad but he is just. Virtue is rewarded but evil behavior is punished.

The hill should be visited solely to make a gift to god. People have made an altar over the years. One part of the altar belongs to the pre-Hispanic era. It is a sort of cave where offerings of cacao beans can always be found as well as candles, copal and flowers dedicated to the Lord of the Mountains. There is also another altar, it is Christian in character, and contains three crosses, an image of the Virgin of Guadalupe, the Patron of Mexico, and three slabs of stone for the purpose of holding the gifts of the people. These are invariably the same sort of gifts: cacao, flowers, copal and candles.

The gifts are for the same purpose: to pray for someone's health, good harvest, protection from evil, blessings on someone or on the family of the faithful.

When bringing the gifts, it is necessary to observe the five days of abstinence in all respects. The prayers on the mountain are serious business as the health, or the life, of the person is the quid pro quo. If abstinence is not observed, then the healing stops and the offers are rejected. In the most serious cases, abstinence may have to be observed for as long as 53 days. In those cases, an offer which is called the "Magic package" is the gift. It consists of *papagallo* or macaw feathers, cacao, hen or dove eggs, copal, maize and it all is wrapped in banana leaves. It is deposited on the altar with a special ceremony with prayer for its special wish.

All the members of the family must observe the abstinence, not only the patient and the healer.

The Magic package is good for all possible boons one might wish for: prosperity, good harvest, anything. But when you use it, it carries an obligation for abstinence of 53 days. A violation could cause the death of one of the members of the family. The Elementals of the earth take matters into their own hands.

The offers of gifts in exchange for favors and abstinence of 53 days is called a Promise. Promises can also be made with less rigorous abstinence, such as 28 and 4 days. All of these are gifts and promises that are part and parcel of a ceremony with the Holy Children.

All the requests are made though prayer. Prayer is essential in a setting where the Mountain is a bridge between the two realities, the two worlds, the two dimensions. One is the earth and the other is heaven, the House of God. In a sense, the *Chicon* is the intermediary for the Mazatecs before the Eternal Father, *Nina*.

The Hill of Worship is an Altar, a consecrated place, a temple, and a Magic Mountain. It can be a terrible and a generous mountain at the same time. It all depends on the state of the soul of the pilgrim. If clean, sincere and full of devotion, the mountain fills the pilgrim with blessings. In the opposite case, the person is attacked and harassed.

It is the power of God that manifest on this place. All the spirits that live in the mountains have their own mission, their place in the Universe. They must obey the Supreme Will, just like the rest of us. When you visit the Hill of Worship, you will meet with the most sacred mystery and spirit.

AT THE HILL OF WORSHIP

Holy Mountain, temple of prayer,
Tears, rituals and gifts.
Your silence is enchanted,
Music of the spirits,
Choirs of angels.

Holy Mountain, Altar of God.
Temple of the Holy Children,
Enchanted place, Mountain of mystery.
Mountain of the Lord,
My heart is my gift, heavenly father.

Thank you solar mountain
Thank you messenger hummingbird.
Thank you Royal eagles.
Thank you Huautla, thank You Holy Children.
Thank You God the Father…

30. THE WHITE DOG OF *CHICON*

A young man named Cristobal and some of his friends decided one day to go to the Hill of Worship. They were all young students who had no inkling of what was required of them. They brought absolutely nothing in the way of the gifts, only beer that they had planned to consume on a pleasant afternoon. Even though they were Mazatecs, they had no respect for the place or its tradition.

When they were coming down, at dusk, Cristobal found a beautiful white dog. It looked like a wolf, certainly not a stray. The dog grabbed his attention so, that he forgot where he was going. While his friends continued to go down the mountain, he stayed with the dog. His friends shouted at him to go down and told him not to delay.

As time passed, they realized that he was not coming. They shouted at him and whistled, but he did not come. He was now looking intently at the white dog and caressing his fur.

The dog looked at him with obvious intelligence. Cristobal was totally absorbed by the dog, talking with him. No one found out what he said, what they said. Time was standing still for Cristobal, he could think of nowhere else to go. The only thing that mattered to him was the dog. He could hear familiar noise in the distance but it was only a nuisance which he successfully ignored. It was his friends who were now worried because night was beginning to fall and whatever respect they lacked for the Mountain; they also were familiar with the legend not to go too far. But they already had.

Finally, they all returned to the place where Cristobal had stopped and dragged him away. He could not speak of any other thing except the dog, its beauty and intelligence. He lost interest in everything else, his studies, his girlfriend, and his friends. He felt a great nostalgia and a great need to return to the dog. He could only talk about returning to the Mountain and finding the white dog.

He did return to the mountain, but did not find the dog. He lost his appetite and started to miss school regularly. He began to lose strength. Worried, his family decided to take him with a healer.

The healer utilized the ceremony of the Holy Children and realized that he had to claim the soul of the patient. First he had to find the place where the soul had been trapped. He spoke with the spirits of the *Chicon Nangui* and demanded the return of the soul. It came to light that the dog was a spirit of the Mountain. He was no dog but a being sent to capture Cristobal. To accomplish it, he could have come in any form. An extraordinary aspect of this experience is that Cristobal was actually able to touch the dog and feel his body, ordinarily that would be impossible.

The healer gave instructions for the family: to take a gift to the Hill of Worship of to observe abstinence for thirteen days. Cristobal recovered and he never again returned to the Mountain.

The moral lesson in this instance is that Cristobal had a spiritual problem that need to be confronted and dealt with. It happened abruptly in the mountain and with the dog. The dog was not real but it was a real being that trapped his soul.

The power of the Hill of Worship is very great and must be approached with great respect. The best thing is not to go unless you have a business there. Otherwise, you can call up a host of powers against you, which put your soul at risk. This can lead to grave illness and death.

There are many legends in this Sierra about enchantments and encounters with beings from another dimension. The case of Cristobal is typical in many ways, except for the ability to touch the dog. The young are particularly vulnerable, and the stories of the past are more numerous because the area was less populated. Civilization is gaining strength with it coarse attack on the pristine beauty of Nature.

31. JOAQUIN

In a previous chapter, I referred to a healer by the name of Pablo. That chapter was written for a book that was published in Mexico during his lifetime. Pablo was one of the healers that had very strong influence on me, he was a teacher and a friend for five years and he will always be remembered in my heart.

It is now possible to reveal his name because he did not want the same thing that happened to Maria Sabina to happen to him. Better to live in obscurity than to deal with the curiosity seekers, the skeptics, and the obtrusive press.

His name was Joaquin Pineda. What follows happened in his house, about two years after his dead. I lived in his house for a few days after it had been abandoned for several months. The house seemed sad to me, and dark. I was not afraid however since Joaquin and I always had a good relationship.

One night I decided to have communion with the Holy Children in his house. I was sitting in front of the stone fireplace. At the end of the room was the door leading to the room where Joaquin slept. I was closed shut. In the middle of my journey, unexpectedly, the door to Joaquin's bedroom opened violently. I heard steps coming into the room where I was sitting. I saw the trajectory leading to an empty chair where the steps stopped, as if someone had gone there to sit. I felt sudden cold on my spine and a little fear. It had taken me completely by surprise but I was certain that it was Joaquin's spirit.

I realized that he had come to visit and say hello, to chat as we had done during his lifetime. It was a signature, as if saying:

-Here I am, still "alive" and kicking. Just want to know how you are...

The Holy Children made it possible for me to realize that he still lives, in a place unknown to us, but still connected to the house that he inhabited during his lifetime.

I could mentally speak with him. He was the same, with his humor and jokes, his guitar and his folk songs, his laugh. He came close to talk with me but did not harm. He told me about his life after death, where he is still a shaman. I should clarify that I did not invoke his spirit, but he of his own accord manifested in the room. Only someone who has had similar experiences can understand the impact of such encounter and the sensations involved.

Through the Holy Children I have learned that the Dead do not die, but continue to live in a different plane or dimension. There are times when bridges can be crossed between the two worlds and the Dead can manifest in our plane. Of course, I am talking from our point of view.

The right thing to do in these instances is to pray for the eternal rest of the spirit, that they be granted divine peace and communion with the Godhead. It is necessary that they pass through the individual tests and conditions on their way to blessed state in the Kingdom of God.

The Mazatec custom on behalf of the Dead is to pray forty days for the forgiveness of their sins. Other cultures also pray for the Dead, such as the Tibetan monks who guide the spirit of the Dead by means of mantra prayer.

The Mazatec shamans are also alert to these manifestations which tend to occur during ceremonies with the sacred mushrooms. They are usually indicated by signs, such as the change in the shape of the fire, or unusual noises inside or outside the house. In some ceremonies which I witnessed with Joaquin, the wood in the roof or the walls made heavy stress noises. He used to tell me that those were the spirits of people who had died in accidents and he had come looking for help. Joaquin would then burn more copal and say a prayer for their rest.

Years later I returned to live in his house. I realized that he had left a tunnel which crosses over from his dimension to ours and he continues to come to talk from time to time. In our case, friendship has survived physical death. He continues as before.

THE LIVING STONE

I am a stone, alive, white and returning
To the womb of my Mother earth
My bones and ashes shake and cry
In remembrance of my childhood, my parents, my first love.

My hopes and illusions now seem trivial, temporary
Far away fragments of my imagination,
Like stars in a dream lost in the distance of time.

My life was temporary burst,
A little star traversing infinite space.
Eternity covers me with its shroud of silence and stars.

Once I was root, a young shoot,
A tree yielding flowers and fruit.
Now I am entombed in a dark silence
Within my Mother the Earth,
Who lovingly prepares the way
To my Father in Heaven.
The Eternal Spirit gave me the light,
and with His Love, my life.

Wait, the Spirit said,
It´s not time yet.
You have to forgive yourself
In order to be forgiven.
Return to your world
And beautify it with Love.

You have many paths to walk,
Much fruit to give, many words to say,
Dreams to create,
Your work is not unfinished.
Lazarus! Arise from your tomb!
Mystery expects you. Walk, and find Him there.

At the end of the path,

> One will wait for you.
> Leave your tomb!
> The rays of the sun
> Will light your way and your countenance.

32. DREAM AND MAGIC

There is a connection between the world of dreams and the world of magic. Once I had a dream where I was walking in the mountains. I found some mushrooms which I leaned over to cut. As I bent over, I saw the mushrooms clearly illuminated by golden rays of the sun.

Next day I went out to walk, and I found some mushrooms! It was not the season so I was surprised. I cut them as I bent over and I remembered my dream.

I took the mushrooms that night and continued my dream. I understood the connection between magic, dreaming and everyday reality. The Holy Children showed themselves to me in a dream. That was a manifestation in the astral world which had repercussions in the physical world.

By means of the magic of the mushrooms, one can enter the astral world without losing one´s connection to the physical. One can perceive both dimensions simultaneously.

Another example of magic dreaming is when I dreamt that I was walking in the streets of Jerusalem. I could see a great wall made of stone. In the distance, the wall lost height until it reached a height of about six and a half feet. I saw a stone paved street coming down from the hill. It was filled with people who looked like Arabs to me by the way they were dressed. The image was very crisp and clear, not cloudy nor vague at all. When an Israeli tourist came to Huautla a few months later, I had the opportunity to meet and talk with her.

I told her about my dream and drew for her the places I had seen in my dream, particularly the stone paved street. She told me that the street exists in Jerusalem!

It is necessary to understand that in dreams, our astral body leaves the physical body behind and travel without the encumbrance of the physical. This astral body can cover great distances that way and see places quite clearly.

Another aspect of shamanic magic is that one view one´s dreams and literally play them like video disks. You can do that with any event in your life, once you find it in memory, it can be thrown on a screen and played over and over.

Unexpected events can also occur, like strange noises, objects moving their own volition, sudden changes in the flame of the candles. Experienced shamans consider these incidents as the letters of a secret language. They learn to interpret the signs with accuracy.

In one of the ceremonies of Doña Julieta which I witnessed, she was treating a young man from Guadalajara. At one point, the roof of the house began to sound as if it were being hit by a giant hammer. Outside, dogs began to bark and howl. Dogs and other animals can see spirits at night and they bark and howl at the prowlers.

Doña Julieta without losing a beat threw holy water into the face of the young man. When she finished, the noise on the roof stopped and the dogs quit barking. Some will find the details of this incident pure coincidence but they ignore that all is connected in the Universe and magic makes this manifest.

The Universe is not a place where separation exists, where "you" and "I" are two separate persons, people, animals, rocks, stars, plants and galaxies are all connected in an infinite ocean where all beings literally flow into each other.

We live in an illusory world where our individual consciousness sets us apart from the rest of the Universe. This illusion is broken in a sacred journey and makes us realize that there is no such thing as "inside me" or "outside me". Consequently, everyday consciousness is linked to dream consciousness and merely mirrors the cosmic connection.

The world of dreams, the dimension where magic operates and the physical reality of everyday consciousness are all part and parcel of the Universe and they are ruled by its laws, which are the same everywhere. This understanding leads us to the world of the Spirit.

Another way to look at this is that the Universe is composed of many planes and dimensions which interconnect, cross over, and contain parallel realities. It is all One.

THE DEPTH OF THE SOUL

Who can understand the depth of my soul?
Who can share in the greatness of my solitude?
Who feels the beauty of Love?
Only you Lord, my God.

My wandering soul walks through the path
Of Love and Mystery among mountains and woods,
Away from the world of civilization,
In the Light of Your Presence, My Lord, My God.

Now I know, oh, Lord. You are present
In the atom and the cell,
You vibrate at the core of all that lives,
You exist in the center of the sun and stars
And you lie hidden in the depth of the soul.

33. THE *NAHUAL* ON THE WAY TO TUXTEPEC

The Hill of Worship was invaded once by engineers and workers, who came to build a road through the home of *Nindo Tocosho* As soon as work on the road began, and the workers began to bring machinery, dead animals began to appear in the mornings. They were half eaten; their entrails had been devoured as if coyotes had been at them.

At first, people thought that a wild beast had come into the region, but the animals were always found near the work area. The local shamans began to investigate what was going on and concluded that the lord of The Mountains had been angered by the profanation of his holy ground. They concluded that a plague of *nahuales* had been let loose in the region to punish the intruders.

The nahuales are practitioners of black arts who turn into animals. Part of the legend of the Lord of the Mountains nevertheless is that the coyotes also obey him. It is clear that regardless of what method is used to drive home the message, it is dangerous to invade a sacred place without the proper offer. The spirits are powerful, particularly the Lord of the Mountains, and grave consequences can be brought upon oneself for breaking the rules.

The strangers did not know these rules or the forces that they were playing with. But the strange happenings were palpably clear to the locals. The consequences were being paid by them. The engineers simply loosened the mysterious powers and left. The people were left behind with the consequences of malevolent beings who wreaked revenge for the profanation. One of the workers told me about what he witnessed:

-I was in the project and I swear that the strangest things happened, things that were not supposed to happen. We had accidents; the machinery failed to work or became disabled. They used to get muddy to such a degree that we could not proceed with the work. The worst was when half eaten beast began to appear on the ground, at the edge of the road or in the neighboring ranches. I felt very strongly that something was terribly wrong. I quit my job. It paid well and I needed the money, but I did not want to catch any punishment.

The shamans took it upon themselves to make propitiatory offers to *Nindo Tocosho* for the sins of the project and only through concerted prayer they were able to bring the plague of nahualism to a halt. They made their offerings directly to the Lord of the Mountains and considered it a success that even though the road had been built, the strange happenings ended. But the harvested crops like coffee and maize were no longer of the same quality and size as before. Subsequent cyclical droughts are now more severe. Some people say that the lord of the Mountains is not longer there.

34. THE LORDS OF THE WATER: *CHICON NANDA*

Several young men went to have communion with the Holy Children in a secluded mountain cabin, but they not know the ritual and did not make a proper offer of cacao. A violent storm loosened in the area and they felt how their little cabin had been taken by the Lords of the Water. For several hours they saw the cabin floating towards the sea. They all had the same vision.

They saw their cabin turn into a boat at sea, and the thought of the Great Flood came to their mind. They heard the violent winds whipping against the sides of the boat and they claim that they also heard the wailing song of sea sirens. They were taken by the Lords of the water and knew their world.

The cabin returned slowly back to its original place and was deposited on the mountain. They all felt the same jolt as the cabin landed on the ground.

They all had the same experience and the happenings related here is something in which they all shared. This is an example of the force which the Holy Children bring to bear on the participants who can be led gently into their journeys or forcefully abducted into unknown dimensions by magic.

I knew a healer in Huautla, her name was Bertha. People called "Ma Bertha".
A friend of mine told a story about her. She invoked the aid of the lords of the water to heal a patient with sea water. During the healing, my friend saw the sea reach the doors of the cabin where they were situated and he saw the waters enter the cabin. They all felt the water and saw it reach a height of three feet. Later, Ma Bertha retired the waters of the sea back to their original shores and they disappeared. The patient healed.

Shamanism knows no bounds, only the restrictions imposed by the mind of the practitioner because the participants see and feel the things invoked by the shaman. Within the world of magic there are so many possibilities of events that all the limitations of the physical world are transcended. You can raise the dead, or breathe under water; you can walk on the surface of the sun without feeling pain or burns, or bring the sea to a cabin in the mountains.

I saw a ceremony where the patient grew long fangs like a vampire. We all saw them and Ma Bertha told me that he had been bewitched. She took the steps to heal him from his condition and at the end of the ceremony his face returned to its original form and fangs disappeared.

I saw another instance with Joaquin where a child *nahual* turned into a cat. Although he did not become an animal form, his mannerisms were those of a cat: he meowed, scratched and made feline noises. Joaquin told me to hold him forcefully, without fear and to eat cacao just as he was doing. Joaquin healed the little boy just by eating the cacao. After a few hours and several instances of force feeding him the cacao beans, the boy calmed down and returned to his normal state. Joaquin told me that the soul of the boy was rescued on time since the gods were taking his soul away.

35. THE WITCHES OF SAN MATEO

Two friends of mine came from Mexico City with the purpose of experimenting with the sacred mushrooms and ran into some extraordinary experiences. Their names are Rogelio and Jose Luis. They told me the next story:

"We entered San Mateo town in the afternoon. A woman whom we did not know offered to make a ceremony for us and we readily accepted. She took us to her house and offered us an adobe room for us to stay. She gave us the mushrooms and lit the candles. When we entered into our trip, the flames of the candles became small and blue. From underneath the straw cover we were sitting on, a tarantula emerged. It walked across the floor of the room. The woman began to laugh in a strange manner. A guitar suddenly came out flying of nowhere and crashed against the wall, without breaking of sustaining a single crack.

"My friend and I left the hut scared out of our wits. Outside, there was a young boy, the woman's son we thought, and he was killing a hare with a knife, and he was laughing.

"When we crossed the yard, we ran right into the woman, the same woman we had just left in the room, and she was surrounded by other women. They were all dressed up in black and looked very strange. They lifted up their skirts, and their legs looked like hen's legs.

"They were laughing at us. And their laughter sounded like the crackle of hens in a barn. It was laughter mixed with sounds from a barn. We were terrified and started to run through the streets. We tried to get to the church. WE both felt an invisible barrier that prevented us from getting any closer to the church. We began to pray then there and finally, we were able to enter the yard of the church. We stayed inside the yard of the church the whole night and we were able to keep the witches away.

"The next day, we left for Mexico City. It was the worst experience in my life. It still brings me chills just from remembering it."

The interesting part of this story is that both saw and felt the same things. Even after the passage of time, their faces showed fear from the experience.

One could think that the effect of the mushrooms in the consciousness is mere hallucination. But the experience has complete synchronism and both participants describe the same events in detail.

The Sierra has many stories about *nahualism* that is a form of witchcraft that enables the person to turn into an animal. Regardless, the Mazatecs recognize that among them, live people who practice black arts and who are *"brujos"* or *"brujas"*, or *"nahuales."* The people are terrified of them. They live in a spiritual conflict with the healers, who often have to counter their evil doings in order to heal people. But when the healers succeed, the evil turns on the witches, making them sick and even killing them.

If a *nahual* turned himself into a coyote and the coyote were shot, say in a vulnerable area, the next day the *nahual* could end up dead from a bullet in the same place as the coyote.

The case of Rogelio and Jose Luis, it is necessary to remember that the mushrooms are serious business. You should never put yourself in the hands of someone whom you don't know.

The evil witches who appear in the stories and legends do exist. They seem fanciful but they are real. To be attacked by one of them has to be the worst personal experience there is. One must always be prepared.

There is a simple defense against these attacks. Prayer is a powerful deterrent and an effective defense. The witches of San Mateo demonstrate to our friends that magic is real, that black magic is dangerous, and that prayer is effective and redeeming.

I myself had an experience. Once I knew a lady who always greeted everybody with courtesy. Wherever she ran into people in the street, she would always find something to say to pass the time away and make friends. One day she asked me to her house to have some coffee. She was between fifty or sixty years old. IT was hard to tell due to the fact that with the hard life of the villages, people do age.

We sat in her kitchen which also doubled as a dining room; and we sat down to drink coffee and talk. Everything seemed normal until she offered to show me her house. Without any possibility of protest on my part, she took me to the next room where she had a large number of lizards hanging from the ceiling in all states of death. Some were already mummified; others looked like they had just died. They were all sizes.

When I asked why she had them, she answered calmly that they were for decoration!

I thought she was kidding. Frankly, I thought she had lost her mind when she sat on a rocking chair among her hanging lizards and began to sing.

I was beginning to feel strange and ill at easy. She continued to sing and started to comb her hair. I thought that the best thing was for me to leave and said words to the effect. I thanked her for the coffee and turned around to go.

She continued singing and combing her hair, without answer me. I walked all the way to my house but I was nervous. I began to reflect on what I had seen and I understood that she was not a crazy woman. She as a witch...

The next time I met her on the street she greeted me very nicely and said:

-Last night I almost killed my enemy, a witch who turns into a little animal trapped her in my room and would have killed her, but she was swift enough to go through the cracks in the roof...

I walked away without saying a word. After I had almost forgotten this incident, I went to dine with some friends one night and left my house shut. When I returned and lit the candle, I saw an animal that looked like a giant rat sitting on my table. I opened the door to the house and it ran outside. It stopped and turned and looked at me with a strange intelligence before it disappeared. It walked calmly away from the house. I recovered slowly but I also remembered the story of the woman who told me that her enemy turns into a little animal.

The next day I took my story to Ma Julia. She asked:

-Did you kill the little beast?
-No
-If it returns, kill it. Do not be afraid. If it is a beast, now that it knows how to enter your house, it will continue returning and robbing your food. But if it is a *nahual*, then you will be rid of an enemy.

It never came back, but I realized that is necessary to remain alert to the possibility of attack from any quarter at any time.

36. THE WEED CAT

One night in the cabin which is in the Mountain of Thunder, I went to say good night to a friend. We had communing with the Holy Children and I was still under the effect, although already out of the experience and planning to go to sleep.

I walked him down to the place where he had left his motorcycle. He started his motorcycle and rode away. I could see the tail lights disappearing in the distance. I raised my sights and began contemplating the beautiful full moon. I felt totally absorbed by the moon and I lost all sense of time and place.

I heard some noise in the bushes, and I turned to see a stone near me. The stone slowly took the shape of a skull. Although I considered this strange, it did not cause me to fear. I kept hearing noises in the bushes, thinking that it must be a small wild animal. When I saw the cause of the noise, it turned out to be a green cat, which was jumping very lively from place to place. When I took a closer look, it seemed to be a cat made out of the brushes and weeds around us. The cat moved around me and was clearly making all its jumps and movements with me in mind. I thought: this is a magic cat, made out entirely of weeds and bushes.

I am certain that the moon had something to do with the apparition of the stone, the skull and the cat. I was totally glued to the place and could not have moved if I wanted to.

Something within told me that the situation was dangerous, but my mind, totally absorbed by the moon, refused to yield. I was enjoying the spectacle of a cat made out of something out of the ordinary.

I forced myself to move and finally succeed. I moved into the house and closed the door. I went straight to look out the window and saw the moon again, but there was no cat, no stone and no skull.

I recognized that the many rules and observations handed down by the shamans are founded on fact. The moon has influence on us which heightens at times of vulnerability. I do not know what the final conclusion had I remained outside would have been, but the images and the beings out there could only be evoked by the influence of the moon.

ABTSRACT POEM

To cull the abstract essence
Of things and beings.

To contemplate the invisible,
To hear the silence.

To feel the surface of nothing,
To walk and reach no destination,
All that I have known.

I swam in dry rivers
Fished chimeras with an invisible net
Watched empty spaces
In an hour without time.

37. THE STONES OF THE GNOMES

One night I stayed late painting a mural on Maria Sabina in the Cultural center of Huautla. It was 12:30 and I returned home walking from the center of town to my house at the edge of the landing strip. I went round a bend when I felt a strange sensation. As I passed, someone threw stones at me which landed at my feet.

My body reacted with fear; I had felt it many times before. It is a reaction to danger where the body tightens up, the chill runs down your spine and the hair on your body stands up. It is not rational.

I began to pray until I reached my house. Next day I went there and spoke to the owner of the area. At first he treated it as a joke, but when he realized that I was serious, he admitted that some of his workers had run into similar experiences. Nobody wanted to take the job of night watchman for that reason. The stories came fast. Someone recalled that once someone had been killed there and legends sprung up to explain the strange nighttime happenings.

There is no doubt in my mind that spirits that own the place wish to keep intruders away. They can only do so at night. But at the same time, it had many elements of concrete physical evidence. The rocks that fell at my feet were real; they had come from the area. I handled them myself, just to be certain that they were not imaginary. All I could tell is that someone from another dimension threw the stones at me but they were not annoyed enough to cause me harm, only to warm me.

38. THE MAGIC HUT

The magic hut is the one where I lived. At first was nothing more than metal strips stretched over a frame with no walls. The stove was made of adobe. The floor was bare ground. A friend lent it to me to live.

I sat down next to the stove, lit some copal and began to pray. I thanked God for the favor of having a place to live. The first day I gathered wood to last for a few days. I built the walls and tied them with rope and string. When I finished, the hut had walls, a window and a door.

I entered the hut, lit a fire and began a prayer for thanksgiving. It was my first night of solitude in the mountains and I was glad to begin this new phase in my life. The copal wafted throughout the little room and I had communion with the Holy Children.

I felt the spirit of God descend unto me, enter my heart and I heard Him talk to me in secret. I knew that moment that the hut was a mansion, that it was a sacred place, that I did not need a thing because I am a Prince. Son of the King of the Universe.

The Holy Children sang and danced around me, they were real angels. The hut became a holy place, a place of prayer and healing.

The Spirits of Earth, Water, Fire and Air appeared to me and welcomed me. The Spirit of the Holy Children spoke and showed its power. From that day many wonderful things happened in the magic hut, for me it has become similar to a palace with golden furniture decorated with precious stones and rivaling the beauty and richness of Solomon's treasure.

This has taught me that the real wealth from the Kingdom of God is within and goes wherever we go. The magic hut has transcended the limits of the rational world, has entered the world of magic and mystery, the kingdom of the Spirit.

When the walls disappear, the magic hut becomes an intergalactic ship suspended in the vacuum of space and floats in the infinite Universe. It is a star that cuts across time and space. When the hut disappears, I find myself in a sumptuous temple from Antiquity. I have many doors to choose from, opening into other countless dimensions and other astral worlds, where bodies are made of spirit and defy the laws of gravity, where the Lord of the Mountains and the Spirit of the Holy Children live, where the Children of water play in the storm and thunder in their laughter.

The magic hut is full of blessings, there reigns the magic light, when the Spirit of God manifests to mortals to cleanse and to heal the soul. The adobe walls become the visage of the Gods of Earth, and they speak with the voice of crickets singing on my bed of chopped wood.

It is early morning, the sun not yet raised. A magic rider crosses my sight on a magic horse cutting through the storm. The sunlight breaks the horizon before the sun itself appears and the barnyard animals begin their cackling and sing the Glory of God. It is the first day of my new life.

In my magic hut, the mystery and magic are revealed once more, the magic of the Spirit.

POET DREAMER

A dreamer poet hears the music
In a magic cabin at the mountain top,
Recalling his long haired youth
And the Beatles music.
Maria Sabina and John Lennon
To Heaven both went
To join God in His Kingdom.

The world shook heavy chains
And the people dared to dream
That peace and love were possible
In their planet and their lifetime.

I now understand the useless wish to trap
Emotion with words,
Bizarre attempt to explain
The All in an ocean of cosmic sparks.
Reason, little islet in the middle of the sea.
That is why silence is golden
And a poet dreams
Beyond time and words.

39. THE JOINING OF JOAQUIN AND MARIA SABINA

During 1995, I spent the summer in Joaquin's house. One night I was sitting at the table, reflecting in the darkness and the silence. I was remembering many occasions like that night, when I had communed with the Holy Children during Joaquin's lifetime.

I heard the chair to my right creak as if someone had sat down. It was Joaquin and I saw his silhouette against the darkness with his familiar brown pants and grey jacked, as if he were waiting for someone.

On my left, Maria Sabina had sat down also and she was wearing a typical *huipil* and her sweet smile. Joaquin had come to wait for her and as soon as she arrived, they began the most unique ceremony, bearing in mind that both already belonged to another dimension. Their joint lesson that night is that they continue their work, beyond the grave so to speak.

I felt a great joy to see them together in my communion; there was no question of fear. They were both, solemn and serious, full of dignity, love and support.

I had a telepathic conversation with them and they gave me some new mysteries. They confirmed for me that death as we know and tend to think of it, is not the end of all. The soul continues to live and evolve in the astral world.

There are two great regions in the astral world: The region of Light and the region of Darkness. The first one is inhabited by angels and saints; the second one by devils and sinful dead men. Almost every single religion teaches this, including the Mazatec teachings handed down by the shamans. They speak of a celestial region and the nether world.

The dead need to make amends and penance for their sins. They need to expiate their sins in the nether and to rise to the kingdom of Heaven only when the grossest part of their earthly living is cleansed away. The Mazatecs offer prayers during forty days and forty nights for the forgiveness of the sins of the dead. The Tibetan monks do the same.

The Holy Children make it possible to see and communicate telepathically with spirits and with the dead.

Mazatec Altar.
Photo by George Hartmann

40. ALL SAINTS' NIGHT: A RITUAL FROM BEYOND

In the last week of October the preparations for the All Saints' Night observance begin. The Sierra felt strange rumblings in its core. The great day was imminent.

The sound of the drums had a marked rhythm dating back to pre-Hispanic times. It seemed timeless to me, calling for the tradition of centuries in the sacred land of the Mazatecs.

The dancers called *Huehuentones,* meaning sacred Old Ones, spent all that time practicing for the observance, which lasts the first two days of November.

The dancers represent the spirits of the dead who come out of their sleep to join the living for a short time. They come to receive the gifts which the livings prepare for them, namely prayer and light. The light is presented on candles of virgin wax specifically prepared for that day.

Every house participates with gifts for the dead. Colorful flowers and laurel branches are placed in arches over the candles, bread, fruit, maize and honey. In many cases the dead are remembered also with pictures of them.

Special prayers are said when the offers are placed on the altar. On All Saints' Day, the first day of November, the people visit the cemeteries to awaken the spirits and to escort them to their houses so that they can join the feast. Prayer is the accompanying ingredient to all the rituals of the day.

A vigil for the dead children is also held that day. The next day a vigil is held for all the dead. The cemeteries become gardens of living flowers and light in the form of candles, full of people and noise. The survivors stand by the tombs of their loved ones during the night praying and watching the lights do not go out. Many prayers are said but the most favored ones is the rosary.

Throughout the whole week the *Huehuentones*, dressed in black capes and wearing masks and hats, danced in the streets singing traditional Mazatec chants. They use drums, violins, guitars and harmonicas for their music.

The masks represent the dead but they also serve to keep the identity of the dancers hidden. Part of the ritual is to de-personalize the dancer so that he becomes a vehicle for all spirits to participate in the festivities.

The *Huehuentones* visit all the towns of the Sierra solemnly marching to the sound of their drums. The drums are quite impressive and can be heard from far away so that it seems the Earth resonates with their rhythm. The days are full of mystery and nostalgia for those that have gone before, a shroud of sadness and hope fills the air.

It is an attempt to covey the love of the living for the dearly departed and to offer prayers to assist them in their journey beyond the grave. It is a prayer for the forgiveness of sins and for the mercy of God, that He receives his children into His Kingdom. It is also clearly a ceremony with the elements of Christianity and native worship with no clear delineation of the two. Indian religious motifs can be found right in the center of church though at another time they might have been considered pagan.

Each day solemnity of the observance gains strength. The climax is on the night of November second, when the Night of All Saints is observed. It is also a night of spiritual conflict. *Nahuals* use the occasion to call forth evil spirits to go out and do harm while the shamans pray for the spirits to do good while they roam the Earth.

One of the Night of All Saints the cemetery is lit up with hundreds of candles and is clothed in mystery and charm. The *Huehuentones* continue to dance and chant with the accompanying music. It is a veritable beehive of activity until the observance is over.

Two nights before the Great day, a group of dancers had come to my hut to sing and dance in order to scare the evil spirits away. It was one in the morning and their payment was food and some liquor. They spend the whole period of observance going from town to town, eating what people give them, and sleeping in spurts, singing and dancing in the streets.

I asked them to enter my hut and listened to their music. I could not stop reflecting on the sacrifice that these men subject themselves to every season without any hope of financial reward, in spite of their poverty, which showed in the simplicity of the costumes that some of them wore. They surrender to the holy observance in body and soul with nothing but their tradition and faith to motivate them, and the love of man.

On All Saints' Night, I watched the brightness of the cemetery from my house, and looked at my watch to discover that it was already three in the morning. I decide to join the festivities and slowly started to walk there.

The fog began to arrive in spurts and the candles in the distance began to disappear in the mystery shroud. After thirty minutes I arrived. I noticed a very strange atmosphere. It seemed like such a small town, the cemetery, full of tombs lit brightly almost as if it were day by the multitude of candles. Hundreds of people of all ages, both men and women, milled quietly around the tombs of their loved ones for the last time on this festival.

Walking around I saw the various groups of *Huehuentones* dancing and chanting for the good of the dead, and I sat down in front of one of them. They were dressed in white cotton pants decorated with mushrooms embroidered in many colors, their shirts were multicolor covered with the ubiquitous black capes. The masks were monstrous representations of the denizens of the underworld. Mostly devils and skulls, but some were spirit monsters, and their enormous hats were made of palm and they made contrast to their music and sweet words in their chants.

Nobody speaks Spanish, I only heard. Mazatec. The *Huehuentones* made jokes in between their dancing to make the occasion lighter, and they succeeded in causing laughter among the visitors. It truly is not a sad ritual, although there are solemn moments from time to time, but the people bear uppermost in their minds that it is an observance of love for those who may need their help to make further progress in their journey through the underworld.

I suddenly felt part of it all in a moment of transcending time, when I felt that the living and the dead can join once again to wish each other well in a festival of love. It is a miracle that through these observances such feelings and realizations can come to fruition. I felt and understood my kinship with Huautla, the city of God, where I was born spiritually and learned about the greatness of God.

The dancing of the *Huehuentones* evoked in me a sense of love and tenderness hard to explain; a nostalgia for older times when this was the major observance in these lands, and I understood that what they do is with their heart, that they enter it with devotion, and accordingly they raise the consciousness of those around them to their reality by touching the hearts of the observers.

One of them had a drum which had inscribed on it the words: "Grandson of Maria Sabina, El Fortin, Huautla". He carried his drum with pride and dignity.

I had the sensation that the spirits of the dead feel nostalgia for their earthly existence and the company of the living, who come to give them aid and comfort in their necessary trajectory on the way to heaven.

I reached the tomb of Maria Sabina and said a prayer for her. I knew that this observance was the evidence that the Mazatec tradition is still alive and healthy in the heart of the townspeople, and that it springs from the deepest sense of religious wisdom.

Days later as the observance of the holiday receded into memory, I saw a number of Mazatec boys improvising with cans and sticks the dance and chant of the *Huehuentones*. Tradition dies hard.

In the morning I returned to my hut. I lay down in my bed which becomes my tomb for my sleep. I am a dead man who, many years before, was among the living ones.

My bones see my clothing hanging from a rope. I sense tenderness and some melancholy for the man who wore that clothing.

Paintings, brushes, scribbled notes, poems, my last unfinished book, other personal knickknacks, remind me with sadness of the hopes and dreams, of my love for that almost forgotten girl. They talk about it with the furniture and the stones, which are in mourning for my dead.

The adobe bricks gaze at the bare walls, a stark reminder of my earthly poverty, which became my vehicle for learning about the spiritual wealth. I truly understand that my passage though the Earth was ephemeral. I was dust, ash, white stone, suffering flesh, a soul, a flame that was extinguished when the wind blew.

I cry for my own dead, for all my unfinished affairs, for all my unfinished work. I think of my most beloved ones, in all that I might have done for them and did not.

They will quickly forget me and I will become another name in the list of their dead relations. Perhaps someone will light up a candle for me on All Saints' Night; perhaps one will shed a tear for me after reading one of my poems. I do not know.

In the meantime, my spirit returns to God.

NIGHT OF THE DEAD

The *Huehuentones* are here already
In the cemetery of Huautla
With ancient drums from their forebears,
With violins and guitars,
hats and masks
to awaken the sleeping souls
with their laughter and their dance.

The dead awaken
To receive the gift,
They come to the fiesta
Dancing and chanting under the moon
Of the night of the candles,
Spirits and tombs.

While the livings say prayers and vigils awake,
The dead dance and cry
Their tears of earth.
They go with remembrance
and sweet melancholy
of their days as women and men
who could see the sun.

Dead and living, living and dead
Join together
This night of chant and dance
When the music quickens and
Mountain shake,
And the holy ground lit up at night
Is a nest of stars.

Sing and dance, *Huehuentones*, friends,
And remember well
That the dead are still living
And speak again with the voice of tradition…

Mazatec Sierra
Photo by Luis Miguel Ávila

41. THE DAY THE MOUNTAINS SPOKE TO ME

The mountains speak and transmit their knowledge and wisdom to us, if we listen. They have spoken to me many times, especially in the Hill of Worship. The voice of the mountains is ancient ant timeless. They call me away to the highest peaks, both physically and spiritually.

By night, they speak to me in dreams leading me into enchanted forests full of fairies multicolored birds. By day, they show me the glorious landscapes formed by the Creator.

When the mountains speak, all is beautiful around me and I reach Eden, heaven opens up a tunnel of light through which I can reach God in His throne; I can see the massive golden door to His palace, which is full of angels.

Mountains speak with the murmur of the wind and the voice of the trees, with the flight of birds and choirs of insects, constantly speaking in a magic language.

The first day that the mountains spoke to me, their voice echoed deep in my heart and I danced in the sun to the rhythm of the clouds for them. That day I embraced the trees like my brothers of the woods. The same magic hummingbird returned with a song of love for a Mazatec goddess, and later a gnome came to sit by me and meditate.

The mountains are temples, they are places of worship and they are sanctified. We come closer to God through them, they are ancient and wise. He who learns to speak with them will learn wisdom.

The mountains speak to the shamans and give them force to defeat death and heal the sick. The mountains teach that the way to reach God is through purity.

They also showed me the brightness and the glory of Heaven. Wisdom is found far away from the world of humans, where one can hear uninterrupted the voice of the mountains and the wind.

The silence within is a state of consciousness that must be developed in order to speak with the mountains, or with the sun and the stars. Everything speaks, also the plants, the insects and the fog. Everything that exists can express itself in a sacred language of form, color and sound, a cosmic symphony where God is the director and the archangels are the artists.

I have listened to that symphony. In the mountains one can hear choirs coming from heaven, as well as the laughter of colorful gnomes playing among the trees.

The mountains are holy ground which must be loved and heard there in thousand ways.

42. CEREMONY IN HEAVEN

Doña Julieta is saying the rosary. One can breathe purity and holiness in the air. There is a lit candle near the blessed Virgin. A bright fills the room.

In this moment, in the beginning of the ceremony, I had a vision:
In the crèche, there is a manger for the Babe Jesus, a white ray of light shines on it. The manger of the Babe Jesus shines with its own light! It is studded with many precious jewels and other decorations, and it is made of gold! I behold the manger of the Babe Jesus and the sight is incredible. Stars revolve around it, and light flows from it without any other source of light.

I see a tunnel of lights rising in a spiral, stars. There are no more walls nor is there time any more. There are many tunnels from which emanate light, I enter one of them and I see my past. When I enter the tunnel, I can see all.

Doña Julieta puts out the candle. She is now a priestess, an Eagle Warrior who can see, who knows and renders advice. She is a wise and sweet teacher.

I wanted to tell her what I had seen, but it was useless because she already knew, she had seen my visions and she smiled understandingly.
There was no more hut and we were floating in space. I can see the Earth from space and I am travelling towards the Sun. I can feel its great power, feel his fire and I become his light. I go to the center of the Sun, I am nothing. The light disappears and I find myself flouting around him. The nearer planets look bigger in comparison but since I am at the edge of the solar system I see gigantic Jupiter and Saturn. As I fly farther away I realize that the Sun is a star among many. As I continue to travel I am attracted by a galaxy of stars and dragged to the middle where stars spiraling all around me.

-Lord God, Eternal Father...You created me, I am Your sun. Forgive me Father, forgive me.

There is a great golden door, surrounded by white clouds, that shines a bright light unto everything that comes near. There is a ladder made of white marble that I must climb because it is the ladder that leads to Heaven. I hear a voice, the rumbling of thunder in my conscience:

-What good are your gifts when the pain of your neighbor touches you not. To be worthy, you must feel all the pain of your brother; feel his hunger and his cold. I died for you and for all, my blood was shed on the cross...

-Jesus, my Lord. Forgive me all my sins; I want to climb to the golden door. I want to be with you, receive me, please. Jesus Christ, help me to follow you, give me strength. Cleanse my soul with Your Precious Blood. Thank you. I cry because I am with You. Holy be your Name.

-Confess it all to the Lord. He listens. Ask for forgiveness in your heart and He will give whatever you need.

It took me a while to realize that the last voice belonged to Doña Julieta, who spoke almost in a whisper.

-I cry because I am with you, oh Lord, My Father, My God. I see your light. Dear Father and I want to thank you in my heart for every single day of my life. You shine like the sun, your robe is white, immaculate, I am kneeling before you and I kiss your robe. Forgive me my Lord, though I have failed you many times.

-YOU SHALL LOVE YOUR GOD ABOVE ELSE!

-My God. You are the only important one! The world is worth nothing no its riches. The true wealth is in your Love, my father of Heaven. Only with you is there eternal light. I want you to cleanse me and to make me holy. My life belongs to you, my Father of Heaven, my Eternal father. Help me! I want to remain with you forever, forever and forever.

-YOU SHAL LOVE YOUR NEIGHBOR AS YOURSELF

-Yes Father I know and I have not done it. It is hard for me to forgive.
I have stolen.
I have lied.
I have fornicated.
Forgive me Father as I am made of flesh, I am dust, forgive me. Do not leave me outside. I want to enter the Temple.

-CLEANSE YOURSELF. PURIFY. MAKE YOUR LIFE HOLY. I AM THE WAY, THE TRUTH AND THE LIFE…

-Yes Lord Jesus. I want to be your disciple. I want to love all; I want to be humble, to keep your silence, to help others and to heal, to console. Dear God, give me strength to follow you. I do not know how much time I have left on Earth; I want that time to be dedicating to your service. I give you my life. Do not allow anything to keep me away from you. Help me Father; I am a sinner, hurting flesh, a soul that cries. But you can make me clean and pure. Make me holy, oh Lord; I want to be with you…

-My soul belongs to you my Lord. I do not know if I live or die. God is judging my soul, my body is gone. Only you live, Holy Father. Life was an illusion, a dream. There is no going back. My childhood, my youth, my middle ages, it is all gone. I am seeing Eternity. My life was short like a shooting star, I am now ether, and I am now light.

-I dreamt, loved, wished, saw the light of the sun. I saw the stars, felt the love of a woman, knew good and evil, practiced magic, and knew the light of God. You know me, Father, you created me. You sent me away to Earth, now I am with you once more. Now I know only you count. The rest does not. It is dust that the wind blows away. Only you Father are real and eternal. Your Love is real. The rest is illusion, it is deception. Blessed be you, Holy Father of Heaven, blessed be your Son Jesus Christ, blessed be the Holy Spirit.

-Amen, said Doña Julieta, who finished my prayer of repentance. The fragrance of the copal sanctified the room, she deftly directed her elements. She listened in silence, burned copal when I felt myself very wretched, and its blue smoke ushered consolation in the presence of the master, Jesus Christ. I stopped crying and infinite peace entered me. Peace and serenity, clarity of vision.

-Good day White Dove, I came today to greet you…- Doña Julieta singing.

Doña Julieta´s song was soothing. She lit the candle and the altar brightened. She offered me bread of the gifts that I had brought. The blessed bread of Heaven, Jesus Christ. As I tasted of it, I felt the love of God which becomes manifest in the ceremony. It is communion, we are with God.

The Holy Children are heavenly Bread, they cleansed and healed me. Doña Julieta was with me all the way, she listened to me, she answered my questions, she is a wise and sweet teacher, has infinite patience with me and God listen to her. She prays for me, defends me, she is my intermediary, defends my case before God. She knows me as if I were her own son. She turns into a warrior when needed, and next to her I feel small. I am now backing in her hut. I thanked her; I told her that I love her. I feel great deal of love and blessedness within. The hut feels like a temple, it is a holy ground. The Holy Children make it possible to transport the room of the ceremony to Heaven itself.

SWEET NAZARENE

Jesus Christ, sweet Nazarene,
Your gaze, soft and penetrating,
Is filled with the glory of God.
Your words, full of love
And your promises
Fill with faith and hope
My sad and broken heart.

You anoint with holy oil
The suffering wounds
Of my soul.
Your voice awakens me
From the deep sleep of the tomb
And transports me to celestial destinations.

I love you, Oh Lord
As I was dead
And you raised me,
I was blind
And you gave me light;
I could not walk
And you empowered me to walk
To your Temple.

I want to kneel before you
And to moisten your cross with my tears.
I want you to wash away my sins
With your precious blood.
The water flowing from your wound
Cleanses and gives eternal life.
Your heart is an infinite well
Of light and love.
It is the new temple of Jerusalem
Filled with the Glory of God.
You are the new king of Israel,
Lion of Judah, and your Kingdom
Is forever.

Sweet Nazarene,
Bread of Heaven,
Lamb, Shepherd and king.
Today I receive you forever in my heart
For you are the Lord.

Blessed you are, Oh Nazarene,
By your love and generosity
You forgave
Those who put you on the cross
And remained with open arms
To embrace all humanity.

All glory and honor
Sweet Nazarene, King of the Jews,
King of mankind.
Blessed you
For you conquered death
To give us eternal life
With your glory and power.

Amen

Spiritual Visions
Mural painting in Huautla,
by the author.

43. PLANTS THAT TEACH WISDOM

The ancient inhabitants of the Americas discovered that there are plants with magic powers, sacred plant such as the sacred mushrooms and the *peyotl*. These plants emerge from the earth to give light to men.

The Mazatec shamans use the sacred mushrooms and other plants such as the seed of the Virgin (*Ololiuqui*) and the *Pastora*, the *San Pedro* and the *Copal*. By means of these plants or plant derivatives, the shaman journeys into the astral world, to seek out illnesses as well as the means to heal the body.

They are magic plants that pass on wisdom to the one who knows how to use them, in accordance with the great tradition has evolved on their use. They heal, cleanse and open the heart and consciousness so that the wisdom and understanding can penetrate the mind with knowledge of our sacred origin as children of God.

The sacred mushrooms (Holy Children) give light for the soul of the person who takes them with respect and devotion. They open the doors of heaven and make it possible to enter the Temple. They teach us to see sounds and hear multi colored music. WE come to understand that all is living and that we are cosmic travelers, but also that we are eternal. They also confer the power to heal on those who are pure of heart and who surrender to them with holiness and abstinence.

We are the heirs of ancient cultures who passed on the magic knowledge of sacred plants. To be worthy of the powers and gifts that these plants confer it is necessary to be humble, to love, and to chosen by the Spirit to be a shaman.

The sacred plants break the mental barriers that prevent us from connecting with our own spirit. The barriers have been erected by modern society which blinds us to our spirituality. The modern world has lost all sense of sacredness, it does not know about the spiritual world. The Mazatecs have kept their knowledge alive through the centuries, by means of traditional medicine and their ritual. The Holy Children have led them into the world of the Holy, since shamans first appeared, during the night of Time.

After the Spanish conquest, the ancient knowledge of Quetzalcoatl remained hidden in the native plants, far away from the profane. Only the pure of heart had access to the temple. This timeless knowledge is our precious heritage from the wise ones. It is presented in the form of dark mushrooms and wrapped in plantain leaves that are with an aspect of humility. We must preserve this precious legacy.

The Mazatec shamans find nourishment in the spiritual roots of pre-Columbian culture. They are masters of sacred esoteric knowledge, which is passed gently to the apprentice.

Many of their secrets cannot be revealed, I cannot write about them because they are esoteric knowledge. Apprentices only hear the knowledge and keep in their memory and their heart. Sacred knowledge has to be learned through experience, in one's own flesh. They cannot be taught. Sacred magic cannot be explained in words, it does not belong to the rational world of logic. It would be necessary to invent new words to explain the subtle essence of this knowledge.

God speaks in secret with him who knows how to listen in mental silence, when there are no more limits and we float in infinite space, beyond life and death, beyond existence and non existence, consciousness in the midst of Eternity.

The plants that grant knowledge transmute the dust of our bones into stardust...

Dawn in the Mazatec Sierra
(Photo by George Hartmann)

44. GLORIOUS DAWN

After having communion with the Holy Children, you must greet the White Dove, the Holy Ghost, at midnight and again at six in the morning. The Dove appears to make known the blessing of the heart.

The healing has been granted and the Holy Children appears to manifest Its Glory. It is the White Dove of the Light of God. It announces a state of blessedness, grace and health.

-Buenos días Paloma Blanca. (Good morning White Dove.)

The love of God.

The glorious dawn is the opportunity to see the sun rise every morning, and concludes the communion with the Holy Children and the cleansing of the spirit and heart. It is the glorious dawn to see each new day full of hope, it is to have a soul illuminated by the light of God, and it is the love of God within.

The Holy Ghost within your heart that is the glorious dawn in the first day of a new life full of knowledge and understanding, holiness, for which I thank the father every day when the first rays of the sun kiss my forehead and I turn bless the creator.

-Thanks be to God in heaven for each dawn that I am near Him. I thank you Father almighty for the grace of having the Mazatec tradition, Maria Sabina and all her colleagues, for the mountains and the cold, for the hunger and the fear, for the ecstasy. Thank you for the Holy Children, for the healing, the miracles and the magic.

-Thank you Father Almighty for the children and the old, for the secrets of which I am now a participant, for the predecessors.

The plants, the trees, the wild beasts; the eagles, the clouds and the mountains sing their hymn to the Creator.

-Thank you Holy Father for letting me hear that hymn. You know that I was born spiritually in Huautla. As here I knew You for the first time, God the Father. Since then I have walked the Magic Mountains knowing that you are besides me, protecting me and blessing me forever and ever.

        NAXHECAJTHECHILI NINA
             GRACIAS DIOS
          THANKS BE TO GOD

45. THE POWER OF FAITH, PRAYER AND FASTING

Through years of personal experience and the teachings of Mazatec shamans I have learned the power of fasting when combined with faith and prayer. There are wonderful benefits from fasting which reflect on our consciousness and our well being.

When it is a voluntary sacrifice offered to God, it becomes an offering of great value in receiving answers to prayers as it cleanses and purifies the body and soul, and by so doing it opens the doors to heaven and brings the spirit within our reach.

By means of fasting we expel all negative energy and it is possible to achieve a sublime state of consciousness. But fasting is not enough; it must be accompanied by faith and prayer. The three, simultaneously manifested, effect the cleansing of the soul.

Faith, prayer and fasting are a wonderful formula of internal alchemy. Fasting cleanses, heals and sanctifies. It is a way which purifies us in order to have access to the Temple Within that is in the heart, which has the sacred doorway.

By means of fasting, faith and prayer we climb a long ladder which leads to the Temple of the Heart. We knock on the door and, provided we are pure and clean, the door opens and we can then enter the sanctuary. The Holy Ghost reigns there, I AM in each one of us. There we find light, holiness and love. Only those who have a clean heart, a sanctified soul and a sincere heart will be able to enter the temple.

In the Temple, the only offering is the sacrifice of love. Fasting opens the path. Faith opens the horizon, the sky clears up and the sun shines through. Prayer is an invocation for a response. The Holy Ghost responds with initiation into the sacred mysteries of wisdom, plenty and ecstasy.

Fasting is an offering of holiness. Prayer is the way to invoke the Holy Ghost. Faith strengthens us internally to walk along the way of sacred wisdom.

In the Heart of the Temple burns the flame of the Holy Ghost, which infuses our soul with brightness.

All who offer fasting as a sacrifice must be a secret between the petitioner and God; no other person must know that you are fasting. The fasting must be for a minimum of twelve hours. Depending on the physical condition of the petitioner, it could be for twenty-four hours or more. No substance, neither juices nor soups, which strengthens the body may be taken, only water or tea.

I can personally vouch for its effectiveness when I have prayed for great changes in my condition in life.

46. JOURNEY THROUGH THE SOLAR SYSTEM

I am in my hut and I close my eyes. My adobe hut is warm and comfortable. Its walls surround me and protect me.

My consciousness expands towards the walls of the hut and I can feel how they become part of me. My consciousness expands by an act of will beyond the hut. The trees surrounding the hut now become part of my consciousness. I can see and feel their roots penetrating the humid earth and going deep for their nourishment. I can feel their powerful trunks and branches reaching out to the sky and aiming for the stars. Their leaves caress my hearing with their murmur at the same time that they are themselves caressed by the wind.

I now feel the earth, humid and warm, the brush growing all around the hut, and my consciousness continues to expand. I now feel the plateau where my hut is. It is a high in the mountains of the Sierra and its rocks and chasms now come into view. I now see and feel the icy water of its subterranean rivers flowing with force. I now feel the earth surrounding me and how splits the body of the mountain.

I continue growing and expanding, now the mountains surround me. They are large and solid; their hearts are made of living rock. The subterranean rivers are their blood vessels which feed the trees on the surface.

My consciousness continues expanding until I comprise the mountains of the Sierra, the towns within, the state of Oaxaca with *Monte Alban,* (Zapotec temples) the planted fields and the wild forests. I am the country, Mexico, my beloved country, and I can see her come alive as a terrible and great eagle, beautiful as a savage untamed woman. Her mountains and deep valleys, her ports and arid deserts, her untamed woods and sandy beaches, the rocks and the fertile lands and her love.

I continue growing and expanding and now I feel the entire American continent. Its sheer size is almost boundless but still envelops me like a blanket from cold and frozen Alaska to the giant plains of Canada, its frozen mountain peaks, and its cold and forbidding forest. United States is a beautiful land of stark contrasts containing bitter cold regions as well as hot and arid deserts, healthy and thick forests, mountains, rivers and valleys dotted with beautiful cities, the forerunners of the great civilization of the future.

I turn my attention next to Central America and South America with their lush tropical forests and high mountain ranges, volcanoes burst and the giant Amazon flows through my body. As I rise America lies like a naked beautiful woman, wonderfully sleeping, awaiting to be pregnant by the love of the sun. Naked and fertile, timeless and young.

As I continue expanding the frigid Atlantic Ocean shocks my body, the Pacific Ocean is warmer by comparison and caresses the outer skin of thin Earth crust. Following the curvature of the surface of the sea, I rush headlong into Europe, Africa, Asia and Oceania, ancient and wise lands.

I am now planet Earth!

I pause to feel the cosmic heartbeat of day and night. Earth breathes trough all the pores of volcanoes and deep mountain crevices. Mother Earth has given me life and sustained me through the years, and now Earth and I are one. I love Mother Earth and bless her as I feel her greatness and all her details.

My consciousness continues expanding by the same act of will as I turn my attention to the Moon, the daughter of Earth, which is sustained by the energy from her Mother. Like a chick to her mother hen, the Moon follows her Mother in eternal circles.

All is not finished as my consciousness continues expanding and the presence of the other planets is absorbed one by one into my being: burning mercury, cold, blue and beautiful Venus, red and desert Mars, cosmic giant Jupiter, majestic, with blotches of green, blue and sepia, and pursued by his daughters his moons; Saturn's turn, with his brilliant colorful rings and crystal afternoons, sleeping giant, inscrutable and eternal, making time standstill, and following in quick succession Uranus, Neptune and Pluto, where conventional time ends and eternity begins.

My consciousness flips and stands face to face with the Sun, the wonderful Father of Earth, source of the energy sustaining Mother Earth and like a loving Father, directing his rays to all his children the planets. All gyrates in a cosmic dance of gigantic and wonderful proportions.

I am awed by God's creation of the Solar System and bless Him as my consciousness floats in the midst of the planets.

Oh, God, how wonderful is your Creation!

How wonderful your Sun, that symbol of your Heart and your Love, which cover us and makes us fertile.

I am truly gyrating through eternal space where

I have become the Solar System!

I follow the Milky Way, My Mother galaxy. The Solar System is my body and the Sun my heart, the earth is my soul and the planets my internal organs, all gyrating in harmony in step with my father's Plan.

I view the cosmic night, I am part of her, and I listen to the symphony of the Universe…

47. A NEW EAGLE WARRIOR

A new eagle warrior was born in the Mazatec Sierra. The Hill of Worship gave birth to a young Eagle Warrior. I am that new Eagle Warrior!

As I watch the horizon, I feel my wings ready to start the Flight of the Spirit. To be a warrior, one must learn to struggle until the end to reach the Spirit with love, to find the light, to exhaust the heart in each new battle until the Spirit of God is glimpsed.

The Eagle warrior cries but in secret, in silence, learns patience to give love without anything in exchange; learns to sing and chant in order to heal the broken soul. He must know how to heal his own wounds. He learns to give love and generosity to all, and his faith is contagious.

The Eagle Warrior learns that all things come in God's good time. He loves the Spirit above else.

The new Warrior was a child eagle. I gaze at the mountains and my heart leaps for joy as I take full measure of my eternal being, knowing that it is renewed every morning.

The eagle warrior is strong and noble. He has learned to heal the sick of body and soul. He knows how to take flight to the highest spirit planes. He reaches the great white marble ladder, the great temple where the Spirit shines in its entire splendor. He knows what it is to see God, King of Heaven and Earth, sitting on the Cosmic Tree, the Throne of heaven. He knows also that Jesus, the great initiate, will return. He has learned to fly with the spirit body, searching for God in each sunset. He knows how to praise God the Creator, and to love His Creation. He loves God through love anything.

The eagle warrior knows that he must take flight soon, he should not delay. His task is to fly, to rise higher, to explore and reach new heights, to see new horizons, each time farther away.

He is alone but not lonely because within him burns the eternal fire of the spirit which is never extinguished. He praises his Creator with the chant of the Eagle…

48. TO FOREIGN LANDS

It was autumn, 1995. I was in the Hill of Worship, the sky was covered with clouds and I was gazing into the forest. After a few hours of meditation, the clouds became thicker and they began to swirl around me.

I saw the clouds part in the west, and the waning sun's rays broke through and lit up the altar on the mountain. I sensed a strong sign that and important message was coming.

As I closed my eyes, a vision appeared to me: it was an eagle taking flight in the distance and disappearing in the horizon. I was that eagle, a new Eagle warrior that must leave the pair. As I look, I am uncertain of my destination.

I continue flying, far, far away, and I can see the lands below, cutting through the air at great speed. I asked the Spirit: Where must I go?

Another vision: I am now flying over water until I reach the feet of a great statue, and it was the Statue of Liberty in New York. Her torch in her right hand shines for me just as it has shined for many millions more with its message of hope. In my vision the statue is alive and looks at me with intensity. She is a great angel with the body of a woman. My voice within tells me:

-You must go to the United States and go to the Statue; you will receive important messages and will be able to realize your dreams and aspirations of the past few years there.

I could not take it all in but one thing became palpably clear to me then: The Spirit was telling me what to do, go to the Statue and receive there an important message. The culmination of dreams and projects. The message must go beyond the borders of the Mazatec region. The shaman's way must be disclosed in those faraway lands.

Destiny has made me a messenger of the timeless wisdom of the Mazatec tradition. I am a writer, a in the quest of sacred knowledge, an apprentice in the arts of the eagle. I have to fly to the edge of the horizon and beyond to New York.

While I do not comprehend it all, the vision is clear and the picture is sharp. The determination to see it all through fills my heart. It hurts me but I must now leave the Sierra and take flight for the United States.

I walk into the forest and go to my favorite spot, where my tree stands. I embrace it with tears in my eyes as I already feel nostalgia for the things that have been mine for such a long time. I leave the forest in tears but full of love and hope.

I speak to the trees and to the wind, I promise to return with my mission completed, and the torch of triumph on fire in my heart. I will return when the message of wisdom has been spread far and wide. To the Statue of Liberty I will take that message. The ancient voice of the shamans and the song of the magic hummingbird will resonate there.

The flight of the Eagle has started!

Note:
(Enrique arrived to the Statue of Liberty in December 1995. He was living in the State of New York during four years. After that, he returns to Mexico and to the Mazatec Sierra to continue his learning.

If you want to be in touch with the author for comments, questions, or shamanic excursions to Huautla, send an e-mail to: **egrm50@yahoo.com.mx** / FB Enrique Gónzalez Rubio Montoya / Telephone number +52 415-107-99-52)

The author and Lourdes Medal
(Mural about Maria Sabina on the wall painted by Enrique)

AUTHOR'S BIOGRAPHY

Enrique was born in Mexico City in 1953, during a beautiful spring. Son of two wonderful human beings, his father, Enrique Gonzalez Rubio, a very cultivated lawyer and philosopher, and Margarita Montoya, a teacher of traditional Indian dances and rituals. They also had their own theater company. His early environment influenced Enrique deeply, and he became a student of theater and artist specializing in oil painting. Later, due to the influence of his mother, he began to research Indian traditions.

Enrique studied Anthropology in Mexico City and for many years conducted anthropological research with the healers of the Mazatec, an indigenous Indian group from the mountains of Oaxaca. He observed and studied the process of spiritual healing, practiced by the shamans. This research changed his life completely. After several years living in the mountains and learning from the Mazatec shamans, Enrique gained a spiritual understanding of the universe and the place of humans in it, far removed from any anthropological explanation. After some philosophical differences with the teachers in anthropology school, Enrique abandoned anthropology and became a student of the spiritual world of shamanism. He observed and participated in "supernatural healing phenomena", and wrote about his experiences.

His first book, "Maria Sabina and Others Healers", published in Spanish, is the result of several years living with the Mazatec Indians, learning from them the secrets of spiritual healing. His book in English, "The Flesh of God: Sacred Mushroom Tradition of the Mazatec shamans" includes some of his previous work. It is not an anthropological book, but rater a testimony of his spiritual research about the process of healing through prayer, chanting, and the ritual use of sacred psilocybin mushrooms.
Enrique´s other literary works include:
"Shamanic Medicine"; "Shamanic Magic"; The Healing Shamanic Diet" "The Path of the Shaman" (All these books are already published in Spain by Editorial Dilema.)

Podcast: Interview with Enrique González Rubio Montoya.
(Spanish)

casaarka.com

Printed in Great Britain
by Amazon